# A STOREHOUSE OF KINGDOM THINGS

## Resources for the faith journey

# A STOREHOUSE OF KINGDOM THINGS

## Resources for the faith journey

Ian M. Fraser

WILD GOOSE PUBLICATIONS

Published by Wild Goose Publications
Fourth Floor, Savoy House, 140 Sauchiehall Street, Glasgow G2 3DH
Wild Goose Publications is the publishing division of The Iona Community
Scottish Charity No. SC003794 Limited Company Reg. No. SC096243

ISBN: 978-1-84952-067-6

Photo of Ian Fraser © John McLaren

The publishers gratefully acknowledge the support of The Drummond Trust,
3 Pitt Terrace, Stirling FK8 2EY in producing this book.

The publishers also gratefully acknowledge the support of The Baker Trust
in producing this book

*Overseas distribution:*
*Australia:* Willow Connection Pty Ltd, Unit 4A, 3-9 Kenneth Road,
Manly Vale, NSW 2093
*New Zealand:* Pleroma, Higginson Street, Otane 4170, Central Hawkes Bay
*Canada:* Novalis/Bayard Publishing & Distribution, 10 Lower Spadina Ave.,
Suite 400, Toronto, Ontario M5V 2Z2

Printed by Thomson Litho, East Kilbride, UK

# CONTENTS

## To my Margaret

*I never got used to you:*
*always the freshness*
*like dew on spring grass*
*told of your life-giving:*
  *always the grace*
  *always the love in your face.*

*I never got used to you:*
*forty plus years, and still I'd awake*
*to you, and the miracle*
*that you were mine:*
  *always the grace*
  *always the love in your face.*

*I never got used to you:*
*in rain and sunshine*
*constant your spirit*
*lively and resolute:*
  *always the grace*
  *always the love in your face.*

*I never got used to you:*
*deep were the sources*
*of life-springs within you*
*drawn from the Spirit:*
  *unending the grace*
  *unending the love in your face.*

# INTRODUCTION

When my Margaret was first prepared to go beyond a relationship of friendship with me, tears would fill her eyes, and she would say, 'I love you deeply but can never marry you, because I can't believe the way you do!'

I have never wanted anyone else to believe 'the way I do'. Faith journeys, in which people seek to make sense of reality and find a basis of conviction to draw on as they face different circumstances, are particular and precious. Whatever our own standing ground we need to be teachable before bases for living discovered and chosen by others. Growth comes from a sensitiveness to what lights up life for others, as well as from discoveries made on one's own journey, and shared. The Christian faith is not as in a pass-the-parcel game, conveyed carefully packaged down the generations. It has to be discovered afresh. At different points of history there needs to be gratitude for faith surely believed and lived in past times; and gratitude for a new day with its fresh challenges which will produce a new critical understanding of the past and new insights to add to faith perceptions. Jesus said, 'The things I do you will do also; and greater things than these shall you do because I go to the Father.' His risen life, conveyed through the Spirit, enlarges and enhances understandings of what we should believe and do, age after age.

So I told Margaret that I would rather marry her than anyone else in the whole world – even if she ended up as the most convinced and committed atheist in the land. She realised I meant that. It released her. She found that what she had been afraid of was that her love for me might overcome the integrity of her own position. So in her own time and way she took off on a personal faith journey, testing out the reality of the Christian faith, asking the sharpest questions of it, and coming to a rich and deep and joyous belief which was her own.

This book is about faith journeys. You can come across them anywhere: I was leaving a political meeting. There was a trit-trot of footsteps behind me. A nurse caught up with me. 'Tonight's meeting convinced me that I need to talk with you,' she said. 'I share the same justice concerns which you express. But when you speak it comes through that you draw on a basis of understanding of what gives life significance which I don't have. Would you be willing to spend an evening with my husband and myself just speaking with us about the Christian faith?' I did. If the result could be called a conversion experience that was only because they came to realise that, subconsciously, that faith was already their unrecognised standing ground. All that was needed was to bring to the surface what was already there. The encounter provided means of affirming it. I find many people like that. It illustrates the situation in Jesus' parable of the Last Judgement. Those who he said were his did not even recognise him. They just lived his way. That was what mattered.

People express faith in very different ways. Some have the words but not the practice. Some have the practice but not the words. Some by their practice enhance words tellingly. Louis Armstrong expressed delight in God, God's world, and people all made in God's image in music and song – and also by recognising musical gifts in others which he could weave together in the rhetoric of jazz.

This book had its origin a year or two ago. Staff of Wild Goose Publications suspected that I might be a 'learner in matters of the Kingdom of Heaven' who was like a householder who had a store of things new and old which could be drawn on. They urged me to dip in. I did so, on the understanding that it would be an editorial matter to decide what, if any, pieces found their way into print. After a bit, it became clear that a number of the essays and reflections were cohering and that a book was emerging.

This is it. Though written at different times the pieces belong, or their affinity can be discerned. The article 'Allies and Critics' is originally from the 1960s. 'Ecumenical Assignments' was written as the book went to print. Almost all the other reflections were written between 2005 and 2008, and are 'pre-Obama'.

Thanks go to Margaret Boon, Leslie Cram and Johan Mailer for all their word processing help; to John McLaren for the back cover photo; and to Barbara Baker for all her support.

*Ian M. Fraser*

# Market speculation and world order: a case study

*The financial meltdown in 2008 calls for rigorous economic and social analysis, but that is not enough. Theological appraisal is essential. Faith insights need to be brought to bear.*

*At root there is evidence of a primitivistic trust in magic – the market being treated as if it were like a self-righting lifeboat.*

*There is trust in unregenerate human nature – as if the creativity which can lead to imaginative initiatives would be held back by accountability and regulation and should be allowed to proceed unfettered.*

*The reality of sin was not taken seriously. Men and women in bespoke suits and costumes grabbed for loot with velvet gloves, destabilising society and making life precarious for millions.*

*Biblically this is called robbery.*

*Biblically we reap what we sow.*

# MARKET SPECULATION AND WORLD ORDER: A CASE STUDY

One result of the global financial meltdown of 2008 was that Alan Greenspan experienced something like a conversion. As chairman of the US Federal Reserve from 1987–2006, he had been the most trusted of financial gurus. On the 23rd October, to the House of Representatives Oversight Committee, he had confessed that he was in a state of *'shocked disbelief …* '*I discovered a flaw in the model … that defines how the world works.'* He was not talking of some tinkering with a system, but speaking of a profound change in his understanding of the basis of world order. He was on theological territory but he did not seem to realise it. True, the word 'conversion' was not used but the marks were all there. He had been brought up sharp, compelled to face a reality which questioned deeply-held assumptions he had affirmed up to that point. His eyes had been opened. He looked on what he had previously believed and lived by, and found it wanting. He had turned in his tracks. He looked for a new way, based on alternative assumptions concerning 'how the world works'. There had been consequences for others, whom he had encouraged to adopt the understanding of world order which he now rejected.

What he had believed in, what he now discarded, was expressed thus by Jeremy Warner in *The Independent* of October 24th, 2008: '*… faith in the ability of the free market system to protect and heal itself has gone up in smoke*'. Self-regulation by Wall Street had failed.

The chairman of the Oversight Committee, Henry Waxman, pressed home the consequences of this false world view: '*The Federal Reserve had the authority to stop the irresponsible lending practices that fuelled the sub-prime mortgage market, but its long-time chairman rejected pleas that he intervene. The Securities and Exchange Commission had the authority to insist on tighter standards for credit rating agencies, but it did nothing. The Treasury Department could have led the charge for responsible oversight of financial derivatives, but instead, it joined the opposition. The list of regulatory mistakes and misjudgments is long, and the cost to taxpayers and our country is staggering.'*

It is well to list and deal with these mistakes and misjudgments but the concern about 'how the world works' drives deeper. It requires theological perceptions and language. Changes in practice must be based on a realistic perception: human nature can be the seat of sinful pretensions as well as hopeful stirrings. The concept of sin, absent from these debates as far as I can see, should feature significantly in our understanding of and response to the financial meltdown. When I worked in Selly Oak Colleges, I met at times with colleagues who were industrial chaplains. On one occasion they puzzled over ways of getting an understanding of sin across to basic workers. In the end they saw the need to express it as the 'buggering-up factor in life'. The relevance today should be obvious.

Sin is expressed in at least these two significant ways: a belief in magic, and a trust in unregenerate human nature.

'The magic of the market', belief in its self-regulatory powers, is really based on the thesis that, whatever devilment speculators get up to, some hidden force will iron out consequences. They will get away with their loot if they gamble well, and no one will lose. Those who hold to this view project no real, credible world. As St Paul says: 'Make no mistake about this: God is not to be fooled; everyone reaps what he sows' (Galatians 6.7).

Play is made of the 'invisible hand' to which Adam Smith refers. But he gives it no credence. Rather he identifies manipulative forces thus: *The interest of the dealers is always in some respect different from and even opposed to that of the public. The proposal of any new law or regulation of commerce which comes from that order [i.e. dealers] ought always to be listened to with great precaution, and ought never to be adopted till after having been long and carefully examined, not only with the most scrupulous, but with the most suspicious attention. It comes from an order of men whose interest is never the same with that of the public, who have generally an interest to deceive and even oppress the public, and who accordingly have, upon many occasions, both deceived and oppressed it.*[1]

The tools of magic must be discarded, replaced by the exercise of human responsibility. In his inaugural address in 1933, President Roosevelt stated: ' ... *we require two safeguards against a return to the evils of the old order; there must be a strict supervision of all banking credits and investments; there must be an end to speculation with other people's money* ...' This accords with the biblical conviction that God made human beings, women and men together, to be responsible stewards of creation, to manage it as trustees so that 'the way it works' fulfils his good intentions for it. Ways of fantasy and deception are ruled out. They are evil. The early church ruled out magic as a sinful delusion which withdrew people from trusting God in their exercise of human responsibilities. Simon, a Jewish magus, wanted to buy the Spirit-power of the disciples. Peter gave him short shrift: 'May your silver perish with you ... Repent therefore of this wickedness ... for I see that you are in the gall of bitterness and the chains of wickedness' (Acts 8.18–24). Paul tongue-lashed the magus Elymas in Cyprus: 'You son of the devil, you enemy of all righteousness, full of all deceit and villainy, will you not stop making crooked the straight paths of the Lord?' Ignatius, Bishop of Antioch, saw in the birth of the Christ child a death sentence to the power of magic. Writing to the Ephesians on the way to martyrdom in Rome, somewhere around 107 to 110 AD, he stated: 'A star, brighter than all the other stars, shone in the sky ... Thereupon all magic was dissolved ...'

Trust in magic is an alternative to trust in the living God. It can offer cover for the greed-is-good brigade. The Creator of the world invites us in partnership to create a world order which works. The alternative, trust in human nature in its unregenerate condition, has had clear dissuasives during my lifetime. The elimination of transcendence ('that which goes beyond the merely earthly') in the evaluation of human life brought not freedom but different forms of subjugation to powers-that-be. As a young man Karl Marx had a religious phase which he outgrew; and Stalin, destined for the priesthood, kicked over the religious traces. Marx later found in the idea of a creator God an insufferable limitation on collective man. Stalin both lauded collective human achievement and dealt pitilessly with actual human beings – both *kulaks* and colleagues were liquidated on a massive scale. After Stalin's death in 1953 this discrepancy between theory and actuality produced a new search into the nature of humanity in the USSR and Eastern Europe. Attempts were made to see whether the element of transcendence could be accommodated to Marxist theory. The searchers had found that it provided an essential ingredient in giving value to human life.

When relationship to God is eliminated from the human, there is no restriction on powers-that-be identifying human nature on their own terms and acting accordingly. For Stalin, the truly human person would be the faithful Party member; for Hitler, those of Aryan race; for Mao, aficionados of the Red Book. The dimensions of human life were thus woefully reduced where there was no transcendent reference.

Theology is needed to correct this skewed understanding of human nature. It is the most practical of disciplines. It addresses the actual terms provided by life on earth, asks what sense we can make of that life and what is required of each of us. It sees in Jesus Christ's life an acceptance of these terms and a manifestation of ways of self-giving and sacrifice which make the world work. He often expressed his own theology in parables, using the story form to enable hearers to face deep questions of life and gain perceptions on how to live truly in a struggle for light. His use of parables showed that there is a theology which meets people where they are, those rejected by society, illiterates, the downtrodden, as well as those who find social acceptance. This has been confirmed in our day where basic Christian communities have grown from the grassroots – as in Solentiname, on Lake Nicaragua – and where liberation theologies, such as *Minjung* theology in Korea, have drawn insights from and spoken to the lives of those at the bottom of society's heap.

Theology can also collaborate effectively with other disciplines which are concerned with the what, how and when of created life. To call it the 'Queen of the sciences' is arrogant. What it can do is provide a significant deepening and coordinating role.

At the very beginning of the Bible attention is given to the question of how the world is to be ordered and how we are placed in it. The concern of the authors of the book of Genesis is to explore, in story form, our relationships with God, with one another, with the natural creation. What is provided is not an attempt at a scientific account of creation (scientific method was a much later development). The approach is, rather, prophetic and poetic, probing the depths of the meaning of existence. The first chapter is in hymnic form, the main part of each verse drawing attention to a principal part of the creation, then the refrain rounding it off: 'And God saw that it was good. There was morning and evening the _th day' (day simply being used to divide up verses in preparation for switching the focus to dwell on some other aspect of the created order). It deals with magic in the bygoing. Sun, moon and stars are not heavenly beings to be worshipped in the hope of their bringing good fortune, but artefacts created to fulfil their particular functions in sustaining and embellishing life. Human beings, male and female together, are made in God's likeness and invited to manage the world in partnership with God, as trustees of the Creator's intention for it and stewards of all that has been made. Marx thought that this downgraded humanity. The apprentice who learns his craft from the master craftsman is not downgraded but equipped for the job.

Two stories in early chapters of Genesis deal with the vaunting ambition of human beings and how that relates to the way in which the world should work. In chapters two and three, Representative Man, Adam, and Representative

Woman, Eve, feature. They are depicted as being challenged by God's form of provision for human life: 'You can eat this, not that – it would be death-dealing!' The serpent is brought in, in ancient Semitic mythology a symbolic figure for deceitful wire-pulling: 'No death-dealing would result, rather you would know good and evil as God does!'

The challenge to make a choice between fruit which is licit and that which is illicit shows that it is quite in order to know good and evil ('know' in Hebrew implying 'relating to') – but only as frail and fallible human beings who constantly need correction, not 'as God' who alone can define what is to be what. When humanity grabs for final power, to order life on its own terms in place of God's, destruction follows.

In chapter eleven, the story is about sinful pretensions of run-of-the-mill humanity. This time the picture is of a city and tower 'whose top may reach into heaven' giving human beings access to God's power base; and establishing human beings' name (i.e. identity) as the one that matters and lasts, when it is to the name of God that glory and honour should be ascribed. It is a recipe for disaster.

All through the rest of the Bible there are encouragements to rejoice in and share God's generous provision for human life, and at the same time warnings to be wary of destructive sinful pretensions in human nature.

Jesus Christ came announcing the Kingdom, the whole fabric of created life being transformed so that it is marked by justice, truth and peace. He presented himself as the Way, the Truth, the Life. That life could be shared; with followers he could work in double harness.

Those who pinned their hopes for a true world order on individual conversions have limited that large vision drastically. Cromwell's inept Parliament of Saints stands as a reminder that to be newborn can turn out to be stillborn, incompetent. Hard work in concert with other disciplines is needed to appropriate the insights of theology and make them effective, in light of the terms the world offers for creative human initiatives. Institutions, corporations, banks, stock exchanges need to turn from self-seeking, self-rewarding ways to servant ways. In the letter to the Colossians Paul says of Jesus Christ: 'thrones, dominions, rulers or powers – all things have been created through him and for him' (1.16). Great institutions will find their true role and get their true reward when they accept servant status.

## A just society

Theology's concern is for the living fabric of existence, how to make sense of it and how to get purchase on it to live life creatively. The claim for justice is central, a claim which runs like a drumbeat through the whole Bible. The present financial meltdown has revealed a world in which justice gets short shrift:

a) No objective measurement is made of different kinds of work and how they should be appropriately rewarded when assessed according to their ability to meet human need. The life-work of a roadman connects communities, encourages and supports a flow of relationships between people, enables the interchange of goods and services. It has never been shown that a banker contributes as much to society. A single mother may bring up children in difficult circumstances, not brilliantly but reasonably. It has never been shown that someone who works on the stock exchange and is rewarded with 'what the market can stand' (i.e. 'what you can get away with') has made any contribution to human good which is comparable to that of the single mother doing her best. Who, in the end, 'sustains the fabric of this world', that is, keeps the world going from day to day? The book of Ecclesiasticus asks that question in chapter 38 and concludes that it is basic workers. Those who pull strings to get over-rewarded ride on their backs. Work may then be priced in a privileged group which itself benefits from a culture of affluence and makes inflated assumptions about the value of the work it produces.

b) Much is being made of the mantra 'no bonuses for failure'. But why should one section of society already well rewarded or over-rewarded get bonuses for simply doing what they had undertaken to do? Society depends on millions who do efficiently the work for which they were engaged, without their being given extra for simply doing it. The practice of bonuses belongs to a society which is so far from a just one that the gap between rich and poor keeps increasing without any rational basis to justify the wide discrepancy in rewards. Failure may still be airily dismissed. When bankers met with MPs they expressed sorrow for the way things had worked out – as if they were like farmers who had sowed and tended good crops which had been wrecked by an unexpected tornado! They had taken action which destabilised society, thrown people into unemployment, wrecked lives! Such conduct should lead to confession of sin and amendment of lifestyles. No sign was given of such repentance. Escape routes to continue to over-reward themselves were left open. Justice has not been served.

c) A sin is being covered over which is close to one normally listed as criminal. To take other people's money, entrusted to your care to handle responsibly, and gamble with it aiming to advance your own status and fortune is close in character to embezzlement.

d) There needs to be a repudiation of money-making as a proper objective of human life, yet there is still little sign of that. Jesus' profound remark 'You cannot serve God and Mammon' has proved its relevance throughout history. Restraint of self-advantage shown by concern for the needs and well-being of others is a necessary element in forming a world order which works. What a poor twisted life awaits the human race if money is made the measure of worth, when all in life that really matters comes by gift and grace.

## A more excellent way

There exist examples of alternative objectives in life and alternative styles of living. Some forms adopt a commonly accepted discipline which enables each participant to be accountable to others. They are thus helped to live out in practice what has been accepted as a just manner of living. These exist as signs of what St Paul calls 'a more excellent way'. Here is one example:

Early in its life, the Iona Community realised that, for it to be a genuine faith community, it needed a discipline to keep it on track and make members accountable to one another – as a help to being accountable to God for the way they lived life.

> *The fivefold Rule of the Iona Community is:*
>
> *1. Daily prayer and Bible-reading*
> *2. Sharing and accounting for the use of our money*
> *3. Planning and accounting for the use of our time*
> *4. Action for justice and peace in society*
> *5. Meeting with and accounting to each other*

The economic discipline reminds us that whatever contribution we can offer in life draws on personal gifts and energies with which we are endowed, and we should not make large claims for exercising them: 'Bread for each day' should be enough. If we grab too much for ourselves we take away from others a fair share of what God provides for all. Such action would, at the same time, give encouragement to other people to live by distorted values.

The economic discipline also makes us ready to take relatively poorly paid jobs when called to do so. A check on reality is provided in that we report regularly to fellow members. Regulation and accountability play a creative part in responsible living.

Commenting in *The Guardian*, Polly Toynbee, whose stance is secularist, has pointed to the need to *'flush out tax avoidance and evasion, to close down tax havens, to appoint honest non-executives to company boardrooms and institute a regime built on public trust'.*[2] These would be features in a move towards what I would call 'righteous living' – i.e. expressing right relationships, right dealings, a world put right side up. I wonder if she was fully aware that she resorted to theological language: *'Brown may be today's saviour, but only by cleansing the City of greed and restoring trust will he find redemption.'*[3] Secularists, atheists, agnostics can open eyes to theological insights. When they identify gods and godly features which they find incredible, it may be that they alert us to idols which we had substituted for God. The unconverted may convert the converted, opening their eyes to truth.

At the end of 2008, the outcome of the financial meltdown is unclear. But one worrying possible consequence calls for the implementation of theological insights. The consequence in question is summed up in a proverb:

> *When the Devil was ill, the Devil a saint would be;*
> *When the Devil got well, the devil a saint was he.*

The callousness of financial manipulators, their carelessness about life-destroying effects on the lives of others, their sin in taking their own self-serving ways in contradiction to the way God made the world to work could still result in a failure to amend a system which has proved to be utterly misbegotten and destructive. If and when an upturn appears they may seek again the comfort zone of self-interest, collude in another ruinous attempt to get the world to work on a basis of selfishness, and steer life back into old destructive ways. T.S. Eliot succinctly expresses the contradictory make-up of human beings: *'valiant, ignoble, dark, and full of light'* (From 'The Rock').

Faith points beyond the self-interest and tribal selfishness of those who would milk the world to fatten themselves. It brings an awareness that life itself is on loan and the use of it has to be answered for; that time and gifts, and opportunities to develop them, are a free endowment, not devices for blackmailing the public: awareness thus producing a thankfulness which is grateful for modest rewards in light of the needs of others.

It should be clear that no mere tidying up of the way we manage life on this planet will be enough to get a world order which works. We should have had enough of a shake to be prepared to give up sinful exploitive ways of living and working.

Alan Greenspan had been 'shocked' to find that his view of the way the world worked turned out to be fundamentally mistaken: *'I discovered a flaw in the model that I perceived is the critical functioning structure that defines how the world works.'* He had looked to the self-interest of banks and lending organisations to ensure that clients were fairly dealt with. That trust had proved to be misplaced. The world was not sustainable on such unregulated basis.

There were features of the way in which he 'saw the light' which might have belonged to a conversion experience. Yet when Congressman Henry Waxman asked him: *'Were you wrong?'* his admission was far short of such a confession: *'Partially … I made a mistake …'* There was in this no awareness of the depths to which human selfishness can plumb. Where people grab for themselves, careless of the needs of others, the world is brought to the verge of collapse; the reality of sin needs at that point to be recognised, confession made, forgiveness sought and reparation offered, including amendment of lifestyles. Without this deep-going action destructive ways of living can be resumed.

Is there a final reality which provides a compass to give life's bearings, against which we can check perceived realities? A.J. Ayer, noted for his anti-Christian stance, wrote in the *Daily Telegraph* of 28th June, 1989, about his dying for four minutes during an operation in the hospital: *'I was confronted by a red light, exceedingly bright. I was aware that the light was responsible for the government of the universe.'*

The light which governs the universe can be trusted to help us discern how to manage the world so that its promise is fulfilled. At one and the same time we must seek its illumination with awe, recognising that such comprehensive knowledge is quite beyond the capacity of the human mind to grasp; and with confidence since what we need, to live significantly, is accessible, because:

a) God invites human beings to be collaborators in transforming the world to fulfil its potential, with lineaments of God's Kingdom marking its development.

b) Jesus Christ came to live a fully human life characterised by self-giving and the restoration of human dignity and place – a form of human life which can be adopted by all who are prepared to live his way.

c) That Way relates not only to the life of human persons but to institutions, classes, nations, international associations – the whole fabric of created existence needs to experience a thoroughgoing conversion if a sane and sustainable world order is to be attained. Money will need to be put in its place as a servant, not a controlling force dictating how life is to be lived and how we are to relate to others.

Those who do not take faith and theology seriously put the world at risk. Theology is the articulation of the faith bases for living life, a necessary discipline to bring to bear on major challenges we face in history.

## The meaning of the Eucharist

*Father Ed de la Torre, interviewed in a 'safe house' in the Philippines in 1973, when on the run from the police.*

'One Christmas, a group of about a hundred farmers came up here to demand land from the government. We held a midnight mass. We were reflecting on what that meant and I felt that one of them expressed it well when he said: "The Christian meaning of what we are doing is this, no? At Eucharist we have only a few hosts, only a little bread, and we break it up and give it to each other. Why is this? It is really an act of the poor. There is not enough, that's why we break it up. If there were enough for all we would all get a whole piece."

'Another farmer's observation is even more profound: "Even if there is not enough, we will not follow the logic of the development economists who say: *Let's first increase the GNP. Then, if there is not enough, we will make sure that we first feed those who are strong enough to work. Others can take their chance.* No! We won't postpone the sharing. There will not be enough for everyone but no one will have nothing."

'The whole point is not abundance or scarcity but that we share in a real celebration. We are not just going to glorify scarcity for scarcity's sake as more heroic. Even more importantly, we are to share what there is available in the period of poverty. What is most important is our solidarity.

'There was no explicit reference in this to the Last Supper but I think the farmer, in his own way, was articulating a very profound Eucharist, which I personally could not achieve with all my priestly training.'

# Homing in on reality

*Is there a final reality against which we can check our perceived realities?*

*A.J. Ayer had the honesty, in spite of his own reservations about Christianity, to recount his near-death experience: 'I was confronted by a red light, exceedingly bright … I was aware that the light was responsible for the government of the universe' (see p.21).*

*It makes good sense to check up on the claim that God is the reality behind all other realities; and to reckon with theology as the discipline which enables human beings to found their life on that reality, and reach for a world order which works.*

*Adventurous spirits, from Abraham, through Wise Men from the east, to people like George MacLeod, have journeyed 'following the light they see and praying for more light'. Astrologers, with their little light, gained what Herod, with all the help of the Hebrew tradition, completely failed to grasp. The heroine of* The Queen and the Rebels, *by playwright Ugo Betti, guesses that it might be God's intention to make human beings 'not docile' but tough customers to deal with, grown-up collaborators.*

*Tom Fleming recognised in Hugh MacDiarmid a similar tough, creative perception of human life, too easily dismissed by 'the religious' – with consequences for Scottish Churches House work on the arts in the 1960s.*

# RECKONING WITH REALITIES:
# WHAT'S THERE AND WHAT MATTERS

The financial meltdown has exposed the Walter Mitty world in which financial manipulators have lived, a world fabricated to suit their own ambitions. The real world will not work that way. Hence the crash.

Money was dealt with as if it had substance in itself, whereas it is a transactional device. For gifts and experience contributed to society, rewards on a ridiculous scale were claimed. Gifts call for thanksgiving, not exploitation. Their maturing and honing put purveyors in debt to society. To be given a position of significant service should be recognised as affording a 'pay-back time' expressing gratitude for society's resourcing – not the threat of moving gifts and experience to another country!

To get a viable world order we have to start with the world as it is.

All creatures have to reckon with 'what's there'. Young cubs have to get to know the lie of the land and pick up survival devices from elders. Fledgling birds have to practise notes till they get right the songs which identify their species. Creatures can cope best when they give their minds to the terms set by the world they live in, and accept restrictions as well as exploit freedoms.

To a limited extent 'what matters' is also the concern of creatures other than human. It matters to hunt for food for each day, to care for offspring. But the scope in assessing realities for human beings is on a different scale.

Enquiry into 'what's there' with regard to the life of the planet produces changes of perspective over the centuries. A world thought to be flat turns out to be round; treated as the centre of the universe it turns out to be peripheral. Over time fantasies have to give way to realities. Human ransacking of the earth's resources has to give way to responsible and discriminate use; the fantasy of an inexhaustible treasure store has to give way to the reality which careful researches reveal: that we have to act as stewards of the earth, not plunderers of treasures which should provide blessing for the whole creation and be shared with our children's children.

On this scale 'what matters' is a human concern and responsibility. This is illustrated in the early chapters of the book of Genesis where human beings are depicted as being created 'in the image of God', a marked family likeness which does not characterise other creatures. In a second depiction, human beings are formed of the dust of the ground into which God breathes life. Other creatures are simply formed from earth-matter without the quality given by that special life-giving in-breathing.

What is life for? How is it to be lived? What is the destiny of the creation? Have we a part in fulfilling that destiny? These are questions which we are rightly faced with if we bear the family likeness which animals do not, and are considered to be stewards and trustees of creation, not to work our own will, but that of the One 'responsible for the government of the universe'. It is in the context of 'what's there' and 'what matters' that God must be located, and that location tested out.

'What's there' is related to the belief that God is present to the life of the creation. 'What matters' is related to the belief that God invites those made in his image to co-operate with him in transforming that life, so that a world order is produced which works to the blessing of all creation. When Jesus Christ came, it was to reckon with 'what's there', accepting without special privilege the terms which human life offered; proclaiming and living the Kingdom of God – that is, the whole fabric of created life being transformed. The Kingdom is not a never-never land dream but a concrete promise waiting to be realised. Over centuries people have tested out the reality of God's constructive hand in life. Abraham, in Ur of the Chaldees with its moon-worship, entered into a relationship which he found to be real with God the Lord of all. Jacob, his grandson, moving to Syria, thought he was moving out of the territory of that God, only to find 'Surely the Lord is in this place, and I did not know it' – God became known as no mere tribal God, operating within limited boundaries, but as the One who knew what life was for and who called on all human beings to be collaborators in transforming life.

How does one test the reality of God's presence and power? How can human beings know God?

The Hebrew word for knowledge, *yada*, makes it clear that knowledge needs to cover more than fact-gathering. Knowledge comes also through relationships. Deep knowledge comes from committed relationships. *Yada* is used for the action of Adam and Eve, Representative Man and Woman, when they commit them-selves to one another in sexual union. To commit oneself or one's community to God is expressed using exactly the same word. Just as a lover may gather all the facts about the life of a beloved which a computer can dredge up, and be no nearer to knowing how marriage to her/him would work out, so fact-gathering about God will get us nowhere by itself – the reality of God's being demands the acceptance of a relationship, tested as in human courtship.

As far as the record goes, there is no indication how Abram established such a relationship – just that it was so compelling that 'Abram went as the Lord had told him'. At a later point it is said that 'the word of the Lord came to Abraham in a vision'. It sounds as if the relationship was established directly, not through inter-mediaries. Most often, though, I think, people realise that God is real, present and active because the lives of other people carry conviction and start a personal quest. My own parents were believers. Their conviction that God was active in life rubbed off on me. I remember quite vividly still a significant moment in my life. I was about four years old. I recollect clearly that brother Alex was at school, which you started aged five, and I was not. We were playing by the porch with cigarette cards. At that time you begged cards off smokers and completed sets as well as you could. Alex had carelessly torn a few cards of my two sets. I stomped into the house in a rage, got hold of my mother, crying hot tears and protesting: 'Alex has torn all my Wonders of Nature and my Struggles for Existence!'

The unfeeling woman just stood up and had a good laugh.

But that temper of mine bugged my parents. I remember being told that if I could not control it I would be unbearable to live with when I grew up. Tests such as the incident about the torn cigarette cards kept on finding me wanting. I remember quite clearly saying to God something like: 'I can't control my temper by myself, but I think if you work with me, we can do it.' We did. From these early years I have been known as even-tempered. All through life I have tested out the presence and power of God as 'an ever-present help in trouble' and as a sharer in my joys; and found God to be the basic reality which made sense of created life and gave it purpose, calling for participation in that purpose.

I honour those who have come to the conclusion that faith is a bit like a baby's dummy, providing a soothing influence for those who want to escape from reality and its demands. But to get to grips with world developments, the reality of God – and the sense that God's will for the transformation of all life can challenge, judge and correct actual practices of nations – must be seriously taken into account in our time.

Agnosticism may characterise an honest ongoing search for a truthful basis for living – provided that there is no cop-out on handling responsibilities which require decisions to be made in the here and now.

Secularism may have a 'get real', dig-in-the-ribs impact: a warning not to cover over awkward realities with religious embroidery.

Atheism, in contrast, is nonsense. It make non-sense even when honestly adhered to. It does not add up. To believe that life goes down the drain, and then to live it creatively puts thought and practice in contradiction (as Christians, in turn, by the way they live, may give the lie to their word-profession of faith). There is comfort in thinking that some positive achievements can be passed on to succeeding generations? Cold comfort if they too go down the drain!

Christian faith is much more realistic about human nature and human destiny. This gives hope concerning the destiny of the whole creation. As I see it, we are on probation. The destiny of the human race is to share with God in governing the universe (see Matthew 25.14–30).

# RESPONDING TO GOD

God has the right to ask daft things of people and expect them to respond. For God is God.

I have seen it high in the Italian mountains where a centre, mainly for youth, was being built in about as awkward a place to reach as you could think of. Tullio Vinay was there alone. The money had run out at that point. Work had stopped. Tullio held out his arms to us and said, 'How heavy are empty hands!' He had gone there because he was told to. There was no guarantee that he had done the right thing. I still receive in the post the annual programme of that flourishing centre, Agape.

George MacLeod was disturbed at a way of living which threw people out of employment and had so little justice in it. He looked for political and economic redress. So he went to the isle of Iona, which in Columba's time was accessed relatively easily compared with central Scotland because the sea was a highway. But Iona had by then become a tiny spot on the fringes of Europe, not easily reached. He gathered a team of craftsmen and probationer ministers to rehabilitate the ruined outbuildings of the Abbey. The Second World War was one of many stumbling blocks. He was once found in tears in the Abbey because the whole project seemed to be a wild goose chase. He went to Iona because he was told to. The Iona Community is now a force in the world church.

The genealogy of Matthew, which gives the build-up through history to the coming of Jesus Christ, starts with Abraham. He was not picked on by God because he was righteous. He was picked on because God fingered him. He became righteous and an example for succeeding generations because he responded. Responded to what? To daft instructions: 'Go from your country and your kindred and your father's house to the land that I will show you.' Any long-distance lorry driver would think a company off its head which gave the order: 'Start off and keep going. I'll tell you when you reach the place.'

Wives of patriarchs in early Bible stories had difficulty bringing forth children. Abraham's wife, Sarah, was no exception. A child by her maidservant turned out to be no substitute. Sarah, when past childbearing age, conceived and gave birth to Isaac. When the lad was grown what did God do? Something inconceivably daft. God had promised that Abraham would be father of a great nation in whom all families of the earth would be blessed. The thin line of promise depended on lineage through Isaac – and God asked Abraham to sacrifice his beloved son! It did not add up. But Abraham obeyed. Sarah would have torn his hair out and shut Isaac away had she known. But clearly he did not tell her. A ram caught in a thicket saved the situation.

In later history, God's beloved Son, on whom the exodus for humanity from every form of slavery depended (Luke 9.31), would be put to death. That made no sense – until the resurrection took place and that death was seen to be fruitful for all life. Abraham's obedience could be seen to be a sign of hope.

How difficult it is at times to sort out daftnesses which are daft and God's daftnesses which are creative and have saving power.

Yet, while there are great saints who get prominence, who undertake actions which forward God's Kingdom of justice and peace, the biblical understanding of saints includes people who are not prominent. All kinds of people respond to God, following callings which may seem humdrum, unimportant. The idea of vocation became limited in the Middle Ages. The word came to be used solely for the call to the religious (monastic) life. But the New Testament understanding embraces all those who respond to God. In 1 Corinthians 11.26, Paul makes this clear: 'Consider your own calling, brothers and sisters; not many of you were wise by human standards, not many were powerful, not many were of noble birth. But God chose what is foolish in the world to shame the wise; God chose what is weak in the world to shame the strong; God chose what is low and despised in the world – things that are not, to reduce to nothing things that are, so that no one might boast in the presence of God.' Vocation is a call to availability.

This became very clear at one point in my life. The results of final BD exams had reached New College staff but had not been conveyed to us. A classmate was passing the staffroom, found it ajar, and realised that they were discussing me. He listened – with one foot ready to take off if he were in danger of discovery. Staff projected my future in terms of a succession of university appointments. They were not to know that the Holy Spirit was nudging me, saying, 'Basic labourers are being neglected – get alongside.' This was two years before the French worker-priest movement started. Daft, wasting my training, scary, moving into alien territory. But when the Holy Spirit fingers you the wisdom of men, well-intentioned as it might be, is nothing like so compelling. For those of us who are ordained, the calling is simply to availability, not to a particular status. We all have to do whatever is wanted by God.

My Uncle Bill was a carter. He carted stones for roads and barley and peat for the local distillery. When people spoke about him they inevitably described him as 'far ben', i.e. specially close to God. Was my vocation in ordained ministry any more important than that of my carter uncle?

The bright young lass in the Dunfermline fish shop at which we were customers when we served Rosyth, took the chance, when there was no queue, to say to me, 'It must be great to have a job like yours – doing good all day, every day.' I replied, 'Your cheerful service all day and every day to people who come into this shop may count for more than anything I ever did in my life.' She was mystified and at the same time a bit encouraged.

People respond to God in all types of work which brings life safely forward from one day to another, often without knowing that they are making a response through their working life. In the book of Ecclesiasticus, in chapters 37 and 39, there is appreciation of the contribution of good advisors and medical doctors and scholars. In Chapter 38, the writer focusses on jobs which seem less important. Who is it who maintain the fabric of the world, day after day? He highlights the work of the ploughman, the blacksmith, the potter. But are they responding to God by doing their work well? The writer answers: 'Their daily work is their prayer.'

Those of us who are ordained have particular and important gifts to bring, but we must not exaggerate their importance. The ministry or priesthood which accompanies that of Jesus Christ's High Priesthood is committed to the whole people of God. It is their response which is decisive.

Real, tragic daftness is found if those mandated to establish a Kingdom of justice, truth and peace play safe – when God, the Lord, throws the dice of the Incarnation, gambling for a new world.

# A MEANDER ROUND INTRUSIVE KINGS AND THE CONVERSION OF STAR-GAZERS

The Christmas card industry does its best to perpetuate a misinterpretation of scripture. There were no kings presenting gifts to the infant Jesus. There were magi or astrologers or wise men making an offering of their tools of trade, discarding them before a greater power whom they now worshipped as the true bearer of light and truth. They went back a different way to a different life.

How did kings nose their way in, as did the proverbial camel into the proverbial tent? The story was conflated with Old Testament references. The most potent of these is in Isaiah 60 – the promise given to Jerusalem:

> *Arise, shine Jerusalem, for your light has come;*
> *and over you the glory of the Lord has dawned.*
> *Though darkness covers the earth and dark night the nations,*
> *on you the Lord shines and over you his glory will appear;*
> *nations will journey towards your light*
> *and kings to your radiance …*
>
> *Camels in droves will cover the land,*
> *young camels from Midian and Ephah*
> *all coming from Sheba laden with gold and frankincense,*
> *heralds of the Lord's praise. (Is 60. 1–3,6)*

This comes against a background where evil had seemed to triumph:

> *There was no justice, and when the Lord saw it he was displeased.*
> *He saw that there was no help forthcoming*
> *and was outraged that no one intervened;*
> *so his own arm worked salvation for him*
> *and his own righteousness sustained him. (Is 59. 15, 16)*

God's rescuing of his people, encouraging nations to journey towards the light and 'kings to the radiance', might have been related to Nehemiah's return to Jerusalem in 444 BC to rebuild the walls and restore the city's life. To relate the 'radiance' which attracted king imagery to the birth narrative was too tempting. But it distorts scripture.

Alan Bennett in *Untold Stories* notes the 'king-thing', and is disturbed by it. He writes appreciatively of Gossaert's *Adoration of the Kings* painting; then adds his sense of being disconcerted:

> *It's a painting that cries out to be made into an Advent calendar, though there would be an insufficiency of windows to display all its wonderful detail. And yet I always feel that it's with the Adoration of the Kings that the Christian story begins to go wrong; that the unlooked-for display of material wealth and the shower of gifts, for all their emblematic significance, are a foretaste of the wealth and worldliness that were to ensnare the medieval Church; and while the Virgin, always the perfect hostess, takes it all in her stride, even in this painting, accepting the chalice of coins proffered by Caspar, it nevertheless bodes ill for the future.[4]*

I wrote Alan Bennett observing that kings did not appear in the biblical text but were a later accretion; and that the offerings were the tools of trade of magicians, now discarded in favour of a new commitment. I sent him this extract from Hans-Ruedi Weber's book *Immanuel*:

> It has even been suggested that the 'presents' of gold, frankincense and myrrh were not gifts at all, but tools for sorcery which the Magi deposited at the feet of Jesus as a sign of submission. This is the interpretation given in Ian M. Fraser's poem about the Magi:

> > Magi versed in occult arts
> > note strange portents in the sky.
> > The Fiend to appease?
> > Evil transcendent?
> > – the omen sublime
> > a Child Ascendant!
> > > Camels saddled, tools of trade
> > > packed, they trace a path star-made,
> > > eyes fixed high, discarding their charts.

> > Questions shake Jerusalem
> > (voiceless myrrh, frankincense, gold)
> > 'Where's the Great Lord
> > whose heralded birth
> > displaces the stars
> > unhinges the earth?'
> > Priests and scribes consult, agree.
> > > Herod says, 'I'll bend the knee –
> > > southward hold, to Bethlehem.'

> > Rapt, they face the world's one Light.
> > Changed, they cast before the Son,
> > gold, the seducer,
> > death-witching myrrh,
> > priestly mystique limned
> > in smoke from the fir.
> > Broken is the Devil's sway:
> > > warned, they choose a different way.
> > > Life is begun! The blind have sight![5]

True, the text speaks about offerings. But these need not be like Christmas presents. In a gun amnesty, weapons are offered, discarded to be destroyed.

Hans-Ruedi Weber goes on:

> *The interpretation of the story of the Magi as symbolising the overthrow of all magic appears very early in church history. Ignatius, the Bishop of Antioch, wrote around AD 110 in his letter to the Ephesians: 'A star, brighter than all other stars, shone in the sky … Thereupon all magic was dissolved, every bond of malice disappeared, ignorance was destroyed, the ancient kingdom was ruined, when God appeared in the form of man to give us newness of life.'*

> *The Magi as astrologers or priests who come to submit themselves to Jesus is a favourite theme in early Christian art. Long before the shepherds appeared on the Christmas scenes, even before the earliest portrayals of the Nativity with Jesus in the crib with the ox and the donkey behind him were sculptured or painted, the coming of the Magi was portrayed, from as early as the 3rd century onwards. Some ten times they appear in the catacombs and as often on early Christian sarcophagi, dressed with Persian or Parthian belted tunics and with Phrygian caps.[6]*

Commenting appreciatively on this interpretation, John Davies, New Testament scholar, wrote to me: 'Incense and myrrh were the tools of the trade, gold the profit from the trade.'

Means of manipulating people through priestly/astrological skills and gaining wealth from this were given up, laid at the feet of Jesus.

> *Alan Bennett replied:*

> *August 4 '06*

> *Thanks for your letter about* The Adoration of the Kings, *which does make much more sense of the occasion and integrates it into the history of the Early Church. Your poem expresses it very well (and tells you more than T. S. Eliot's!).*

> *All good wishes and thanks for the trouble to write.*

> *Alan Bennett*

# A PAGAN TAKES ON THE ROLE OF MESSIAH

God works without being bound to a chosen people or church. At the end of the day, someone who had not even heard the name of Jesus Christ might prove to be more acceptable to God than myself. The parable of the Last Judgement makes it clear that it is life lived truly on the basis of knowledge available that matters. Those who prove to be accepted and blessed react with surprise: 'Never saw you around. Where do you come in?' Jesus has to instruct their eyes to see in the hungry and thirsty, the foreigner, the naked, the ill, the jailed to whom they had ministered … his very self. Cyrus, emperor of Babylon, is a case in point.

Isaiah, astonishingly, bestows on Cyrus a title which would seem exclusively to belong to the expected deliverer of the chosen people in the Hebrew-Christian tradition (45.1). Cyrus II (the Great) was an empire-builder. He subdued Media, conquered what is now Turkey and went as far as north-west India. Turning to Babylonia, he annexed the whole Babylonian empire in 539 BC. This vast territory he divided into provinces with a satrap as ruler. Throughout these provinces Cyrus instituted local government in the hands of local people. Exiles from earlier conquests were given the right to retain their own cultural and religious traditions. This meant that some ceased to dream of a return to their land of origin and made their place in the Babylonian empire their new homeland. But there were Hebrews who would not settle:

> *By the rivers of Babylon we sat down and wept*
> *as we remembered Zion …*
> *those who had carried us captive*
> *asked us to sing them a song,*
> *our captors called on us to be joyful:*
> *'Sing us one of the songs of Zion.'*
> *How can we sing the Lord's song*
> *in a foreign land?*
> *If I forget you, Jerusalem,*
> *may my right hand wither away;*
> *let my tongue cleave to the roof of my mouth*
> *if I do not remember you,*
> *if I do not set Jerusalem above my chief joy. (Ps. 137)*

Cyrus noted this feeling of exile and responded. The captives who chose to do so were allowed to return to Jerusalem to rebuild the temple. They were given a large sum of money to enable them to tackle the project. The temple vessels which Nebuchadnezzar had seized had not been melted down – Cyrus restored these to the returnees.

Isaiah acknowledges that this is done without recognition of God.

Thus says the Lord to his anointed, Cyrus:

> *'I have called you by name and given you a title*
> *though you have not known me.*
> *I am the Lord, and there is none other;*
> *apart from me there is no God.*
> *Though you have not known me I shall strengthen you …' (Isaiah 45)*

The instigator of this deliverance is taken to be the Babylonian god Merduk: as far as we know, Cyrus would ascribe to him the credit. Isaiah would long for it to be otherwise. But he accepts the reality. This being so, he still bestows on Cyrus the title 'Messiah' (Hebrew *mashiah*, Greek *Christos*, i.e. God's anointed). Without recognising the real instigator of deliverance, Cyrus still acts as servant of God's purpose.

Jesus was cagey about his disciples calling him 'Messiah': he needed to give the word different content than the power-content which was assumed. Should Isaiah have been more wary about giving the title to a heathen ruler? He was consistent with Jesus' way of thinking set forth in the parable of the Last Judgement. God is free. God chooses whom God chooses. It does not have to do with having the right words or being an heir of the right tradition. It has to do with living God's way.

At the heart of this is a major theological insight. The mission to transform the world – to establish God's Kingdom in and through the kingdoms of the world – remains God's. There is no handover to consecrated human beings. Human beings are agents, stewards, trustees, collaborators. The hand on the tiller remains God's. God acts how and through whom God chooses.

So a major concern for Christians is to be alert to what God is doing in the world, with an availability to be shouted in here and left out there. To pay attention to what God is doing in secret, which demands alertness, is a prophetic require-ment. Amos puts this clearly: 'Surely the Lord God does nothing without reveal-ing his secret to his servants the prophets' (3.7).

The kind of alertness required is well illustrated for me by the Mandela story.

Those of us who tried to make a dent in the apartheid regime in South Africa know how unyielding it was. International pressure and sanctions seemed to have no effect. I once went into a small superstore and looked at the place of origin of all boxed and tinned products. Even the simplest would come from several countries. If one part of the world cut off supplies to South Africa these could be made up from elsewhere.

What hope was there in Nelson Mandela? He had been jailed for 27 years, out of sight of the world. He must have lost heart. At any rate, he would be quite out of touch. Then there was de Klerk, an unlikely deliverer. He was knit into the white establishment. His power, prestige, career depended on maintaining the status quo. But unlikely people were put together to overturn a system which seemed unshakeable. It was God's doing and marvellous in our eyes.

When I went to Guatemala in 1980 when it was, with El Salvador, killing fields, I received a warning from basic Christian communities with which I sought contact: 'Don't try to get in touch with us. We will get in touch with you.' There would be no disguising that I was a foreigner. I would be followed. 'Police or military could burst in on our meeting, pick out those who seemed to be leaders and make them "disappear".' What came after that left the military scratching their heads. Again and again, through prayer and self-offering, men and women would emerge to provide leadership who were the last you would think of. Mice became lions.

God is at work in the world, subverting evil systems. We are called to be co-conspirators with God till the kingdom of the world becomes the Kingdom, accepting whatever instruments and whatever people are raised up by the Spirit to play a part. As Isaiah says: 'The Lord will arise … to do what he must do, however strange the deed, and to work his work, however alien it seems' (Isaiah 28.21).

# ALLIES AND CRITICS

*An article originally from the mid-1960s*

Even the Christian community is too narrow a constituency to tackle the full work of the construction of world theology. I do not mean by these words that I expect one integrated world theology to come into existence. Theology which is contributed to from all countries and cultures will be a continual shimmer of changing light. The Spirit is to be poured out upon *all flesh.*

The Christian God can become a tribal God of Christians – made in their image to protect them and support their interests – if they are denied the challenge and insights of those who respond to the same God in different ways, both hidden and open. Jesus Christ himself, if he is Saviour and Lord, must always be eluding the grasp of his followers, continually confounding them by the surprises he springs, the sides of his character he reveals: shattering the best images of himself which provide the drive for faith and evangelism. Otherwise he would not be Lord. Muslims, Hindus, Buddhists, people of all faiths, must be listened to – not simply to hear confirmation of Christian views or to be exposed to contrary views, but for fresh illumination about the God one seeks to serve. Atheists may vividly speak to us on behalf of many of those who stand outwith the Christian fold, who are essential for its life. The temptation will be to stay where we are and as we are, to get whatever is 'other' on to familiar territory, and deal with it in familiar terms.

In 1964 a group of artists who were substantially atheist and agnostic met with Christians who had a concern for the arts, in Scottish Churches House, Dunblane. At one point Picasso's *Guernica* was explored through a blow-up slide and discussion. 'There you find a profoundly Christian statement about war,' observed one of the participants. A prominent artist rounded on him angrily: 'You Christian monopolists! You can't see anything that is good without trying to get your claws on it and claiming it for yourselves: Picasso is a Marxist, an atheist. That is a Marxist statement about war made by an atheist. You must swallow that, however little you relish it. You have no right to sweep whatever you fancy into your own Christian net.'

The point must be fully taken.

Yet if it is true that the Christian God is not the God of Christians but the God of all the earth, the perception of how and where God is at work outside explicit

Christian testimony is part of the concern of theology. To put it another way – it is part of the prophetic role of Christians to understand the response made in life to Jesus Christ by those who, until there is a sorting out of sheep and goats, have no awareness that they are making any response to him at all.

Alternative views must not be defused by being tidied into prevailing Christian perceptions but freely offer radical challenge to them. Picasso's understanding of the horrors of war, for instance, should challenge Christians to rethink the collaboration of the church through history in promoting and blessing war – and ask whether a Marxist atheist has not stated something which enables committed Christians to interpret the implications of their faith much more radically. The faith becomes a different thing when the eyes and the ears of the honest unbelieving critic instruct the old vision and the old hearing of faith. Agnostics may have a door of escape from theological testimony through their refusal to be committed, but not atheists. Atheists, by virtue of the fact of being atheists, must make clear what gods they reject. The reflection of thoughtful atheists on gods they find incredible should be received as a major contribution to theology. Sometimes their rejection of such gods finds atheists and Christians making common cause. Sometimes Christians are forced to face up to forms of idolatry and delusion which have infiltrated their conceptions of God. Sometimes atheists are made agnostic about their atheism.

In much European and American drama over the last twenty years, human nature, mystery and destiny have been central preoccupying themes. Human dignity and fallibility, sin, guilt and suffering, the search for escape from the grip of fate into meaningfulness, the claim on humans that they live with integrity even when deprived of hope – these questions are central. In his preface to *A View from a Bridge* Arthur Miller looks back to classical times and writes: '*We, now, must (like Greek drama then) ask the largest questions. Where are we going now that we are all together, all in the same boat?*' It is no accident that classical themes are re-used, as in Anouilh's *Antigone* or Sartre's *Les Mouches*. Questions of conscience and personal integrity, questions of sin, guilt and judgement are given vivid contemporary reference against a classical setting. At times classical Christian concepts are challenged – as Sartre convincingly challenges traditional Christian pictures of Hell in his play *Huis Clos*.

One of the main contributions to world theology on the part of atheist dramatists is the presentation of the raw dereliction of humankind and the dislocation in relationships which prevent people from communicating effectively with one another. One of our problems, we who are Christians, is that we come too quickly to resurrection. Even when we think of the suffering and crucifixion of Christ, we hold the Resurrection up our sleeves to take the edge off dismay. In Lent we are tempted to internalise and stereotype suffering and dwell on it without relating it to the dereliction and paralyses of humankind today. If Christ indeed took on himself the God-forsakenness of humanity, then modern instances of God-forsakenness should be recognisable signs of his present suffering.

From New World theologies there is a cry that we take with full theological seriousness the impact of human deprivation today. Here atheist dramatists may teach us something fundamental, and provide a bridge of understanding to Third World theologies.

For we have made shallow the deep graph drawn in Philippians 2.5–11. In it, the stripping of Jesus Christ is expressed, his exposure to all that makes up human life, including its savagery and rejection, his reduction to a 'nothing', his degradation, suffering, criminal-type death. It is only once all this is said and given weight that the graph begins to rise and the notes of resurrection sound out till they reach a crescendo. We have made shallow this graph.

A correction lies in the gift which is displayed by some of the most perceptive of contemporary dramatists – to draw one leg of such a graph of humanity, and let it stand by itself. This is achieved by Samuel Beckett by consigning characters to dustbins and to burial up to the waist. We may not be allowed to hope – but at least we are not allowed to draw the blinds upon the narrowness, the futility, the non-communication of much of what makes up human existence.

In *Death of a Salesman* the narrative remorselessly peels off layer after layer of human self-delusion, and in depicting the reactions of the main character challenges a family to come to terms with their hypocrisies and own real beings.

If we take playwrights like Beckett and Miller seriously, we will be exposed to the full impact of human frustration and despair, delusions of grandeur, helplessness, the meaningless of existence. It is as if some modern dramatists were pulling at the sleeve of the church and saying, 'Don't go into your temples and sing songs of hope until you have turned full-face to reckon with this fact: humanity has a place of privilege and responsibility in the Creation which gives immortal longings – and they die like the beasts. What is more, any god to whom they may call is absent from their struggles.' Remember the one who cried: 'My God, my God, why hast thou forsaken me?'

Yet when all has been said and reckoned with, despair is not enough. We may go back to Antigone. Of her faith the chorus says: '*Antigone is calm tonight and we shall never know the name of the fever that consumed her.*' Is a bright spirit like hers the blaze of a star which is lost in final darkness? We live a contradiction if we live with integrity but without hope. We live in a universe which has no moral significance, no relation to our struggles. We must know the name of the fever!

In Act II of *Waiting for Godot* the dead tree sprouts leaves. As if to say: 'Only if we face up to humanity's utter final futility and doom, have we a right to say that we take human life with full seriousness: but once we have faced up to this without flinching, a barren tree may become a small sign of hope.' May this not be transferred to a full Christian setting in the following terms?: Only those who are prepared to stand with the human race in their dereliction have a right to sound out the resurrection note.

In this light, is the search of Ugo Betti for meaning for humanity's life, from a definitely Christian perspective, so far removed from the search of atheist dramatists? His prevailing theme, says his translator, Henry Reed, is 'man's fatal disregard of God'. In the thick of danger, the heroine of Betti's play *The Queen and the Rebels*, '*one of those very common plants that you naturally find growing out of the manure heap of three years wars*', wins a dignity and sense of purpose which could not have been anticipated at the beginning of the play. Just before her death, she reflects: '*I believe that God … has intentionally made us, not docile, for that he would find useless … but different from himself and a little too proud … so that we may … stand against him, thwart him, amaze him … perhaps that is his purpose.*' Her last words, before being shot, as she looks over the world: '*Unquestionably, this is a seat for kings, and in it we must try to live regally.*'[7]

In this look back to arts consultations in Scottish Churches House in the 1960s, I add this rueful memory:

## Allies and critics (A poem about Hugh MacDiarmid)

'*Him? He's outrageous in his cups –*
*can be obscene, and there's a pub next door.*
*Just leave him out. He needn't know we meet.*'

*I should have closed my ears.*
*What intent should mark an ecumenical house*
*if not to make welcome people who are foul in cups*
*as well as those foul in conformities?*

*And then he wrote*
*leaning against a wall of pain*
*so kindly, so thoughtfully:*
*the poet I never met*
*and wanted to, dissuaded*
*by harsh forebodings, masquerading*
*as Christian love.*

*Who gained?*
*I lost.*

# The world is the agenda

*When I worked for the World Council of Churches, one of the studies being undertaken at that time tended to have the basis of its work on mission described as 'The World Sets The Agenda'. This was inaccurate. At the time liberation theologies were stressing the importance of what was happening in the world as the point of entry for theological appraisal. This was a valuable corrective to the emphasis which began with scholarship and carried out studies which then looked vaguely for some point where they might hook into life's realities. But theology requires a double alertness – to situations faced and to revelation provided to enlighten our way of addressing them. The call to establish justice on earth, which runs like an insistent drumbeat through the Old and New Testaments, may encourage us to be alert to spot new, contemporary forms of slavery.*

*We have to be alert to the character and quality of the lives of nations as well as that of persons. The American Human Development Report is a sign of the need to go beyond lesser development assessments to examine what advances 'the richness of human life'. It allows a much more rounded picture of national life to be given. We need to bring into the open hidden factors: e.g. the role of oil, the favouring and disfavouring of nations, the lauding and downplaying of democracy, contemporary erosion of human rights, the need to get rid of war. The world* **is** *the agenda.*

# NATIONS UNDER JUDGEMENT

Jesus' parable of the Last Judgement is so often thought about as if merely concerned with individuals being called to account, that it is necessary to affirm that the text makes clear it is also about nations being called to account. National life comes under judgement. All the nations have to submit to that truth-revealing judgement at the end of the day. Some nations, using propaganda, will put themselves forward as 'good guy' nations and revile others as 'bad guys'. Such devices will be seen through when nations appear before God's judgement seat. We should not take nations at their own self-evaluations, but anticipate God's final judgement by developing rigorous examination of significant facets of national life which call to be addressed, some of which will need to be put right here and now. For that we need appropriate instruments. Testing situations call for objective research along with theological scrutiny.

A reflection made to me on one of my visits to the Philippines by Senator Salonga, a Baptist lay preacher, stuck in my mind. He spoke of *'the evangelical necessity of research into the development of multinational companies, lest we get into a powerful grip which is other than God's'*. The perception calls for the quality of research which exposes realities which nations might want to conceal, as well as those which are to their credit, as a requirement of the gospel. Change may then take place wherever people have the will to put right what is shown to be wrong in national life. One of the Hebrew words for forgiveness is *kipper*, which has in it the idea of covering. Research can expose 'cover-ups' and lead to just alternatives. When these are set in place the sin will be 'covered away' – like an infectious piece of bad meat wrapped up and thrown into the fire to be got rid of forever.

The USA is blessed with an instrument which can enable it as a nation to come level with realities in its national life, allowing it, if the will is there, to make changes which will enable it to anticipate positively God's final judgement. I know of no equivalent in Britain, but parallel findings may be noted.

In 1990 Harvard Professor of Economics and Nobel Laureate economist Amartya Sen helped to initiate the American Human Development Report.[8] At the time I write, July 2008, the Report, sponsored by Oxfam America and two foundations, the Conrad Hilton and the Rockefeller, has just been published. Dr Sen has described its purpose thus:

> *'Human development is concerned with what I take to be the basic development idea: namely, advancing the richness of human life, rather than the richness of*

*the economy in which human beings live, which is only part of it.'*

Whether he does so consciously or not, he is giving expression to Jesus Christ's affirmation. Contrasting his mission with that of robbers who break into a sheep-fold 'to steal and destroy', Jesus says: 'I came that people might have life, and have it abundantly.' Research can reveal the substance of actual situations, so that they can be addressed – giving cause for rejoicing or calling for remedy.

Dr Sen is also a patriot. Whether he does so consciously or not, he wants his nation to show up, in the end, as one concerned with the establishing on earth of God's Kingdom of justice, truth and peace. A true patriot will not adopt the atti-tude 'my country right or wrong', but will rejoice in what is seen to be right, and want to put right what is seen to be wrong.

I was in the US when Senator McCarthy was rousing anti-communist hysteria. Good Christians with whom Margaret and I lived for a day or two were ready to believe mere rumours about neighbours. They cut them off, froze them out of relationships on the basis of unfounded gossip. The fevered desire to show how patriotic you were was unpatriotic, because it was founded on misrepresentation and lies.

The American Human Development Report shows that the USA, which had come second in the 1990 assessment of national quality of life, had dropped to twelfth place. The eleven countries which now rank higher do this on a lower per capita income. Though the average income of US citizens is the second highest in the world, the US ranks only forty-second in terms of life expectancy, and thirty-fourth in the number of children surviving their first year of life.

What has caused such a rich country to fail so many of its citizens? The gauge of acceptance in the sight of God at the Last Judgement is the extent to which a nation cares for those who are neglected and oppressed, denied the fullness of life which Jesus Christ came to bring. What does the Report suggest needs to be remedied? It pinpoints the following:

- The richest one-fifth of the population has an average income of $168,179 per year, the poorest one-fifth an average income of $11,352 – a differential of almost 15 to 1. The level of child poverty is highest of all rich countries.

- Forty-seven million Americans have no adequate health insurance cover. When illness strikes they are left unprotected.

- A country which has 5% of the world's population, has 24% of its own people in prison.

- Family leave, sick leave, and childcare are at the hazard of local circumstances. There is no federally mandated maternity leave.

- 14% of the population, i.e. 40 million, lack the literacy skills to perform simple everyday tasks such as understanding newspaper articles and instruction manuals. Whereas in Europe, Canada, Japan and Russia enrolment of three- and four-year-olds in pre-school runs at about 75%, in the US, it is just over 50%.

Credit must be given to a nation which allows such reports to be made public. There are countries in which such information would be suppressed. There remains the challenge to pick up this awkward ball and run with it.

One of the dodges is to divert attention by piling criticism on other nations which do not live by the same priorities as the USA.

Nicaragua and Cuba have particularly suffered.

The parable of the Last Judgement provides a warning that the final verdict on the life of nations will mean a turn-up for the books. Nations which preen themselves on their righteousness will get their comeuppance; those who make no pretensions but establish fair and just practices will shine like stars.

## God and oil: a conversation between God and George W. Bush

*In my dream, George W. Bush died and appeared before God. He did not wait for God to speak. Adopting a cowboy stance, he blurted, 'Though I say it myself, I think we worked well together in my presidency – so I'm glad to meet you.' …*

*God:*      Why did you set in course the destruction of Iraq?

*George W:*   Well, Saddam was your enemy; and we had to do something about 9/11.

*God:*      He was not involved.

*George W:*   He was handy. In any case, he brutally oppressed his own people.

*God:*      You mean Halabja, where dissident Kurds were massacred by poisoned gas in 1988?

*George W:*  That's it.

*God:*      Well, why did your father, in his presidency, cosy up to Saddam, in spite of all that?

*George W:*  You must get allies where you can find them! In any case, Saddam kept defying UN mandates.

*God:*      More than Israel? Why did you not attack Israel?

*George W:*  You know that Israel is on your side. You know that Saddam had to be removed.

*God:*      Awareness of guilt is in evidence when a warring country honours its own dead, but does not even count the numbers of opponents killed. To shrug off these as mere 'collateral damage' is to act as if lives I gave held no importance if they were of those you call enemies. You wanted oil.

*George W:*  Honest to God, it never crossed my mind.

*God:*      Don't take my name in vain. Come clean about negotiations.

*George W:*  What negotiations?

*God:*      Those which follow up the pressure which has succeeded in getting Iraq to open up to foreign investors six of its major oil fields. Negotiations are proceeding with Exxon Mobil, Chevron, Shell, BP and Total, to take advantage of this opportunity.

*George W:*  But that is generous of us! Iraq needs capital.

*God:*      Iraq needs reparations for the destruction imposed on it – your responsibility was to rebuild, not to exploit.

*George W:*  But they do need income. The plan has always been to put all this into the control of the Iraq National Oil Company.

*God:*      Then why is this the basis of negotiations: that foreign oil companies will keep 75% of the value, leaving 25% to Iraqis? There is a difference between getting national earnings from national resources and blatant exploitation!

*George W:*    I have always been on the side of law …

*God:*    Under Geneva Conventions, invading a country to purloin its national assets is illegal.

*George W:*    Lord, I didn't know, I didn't know …

*God:*    Among liars I know, you are especially unconvincing. Depart from me …

*George W:*    Come on, God. That's unfair. I have always promoted you.

*God:*    Depart from me …


## A letter from the US conference for the World Council of Churches to the 9th Assembly of the WCC, Porto Alegre, Brazil, February 2006

*For someone who, in travels for the World Council of Churches in Central America, found the USA promoting democracy in words while supporting oppressive dictatorships (a device not unknown in British colonial and modern history), a contribution to the WCC Assembly in Porto Alegre in February 2006 is significant. Delivered by Orthodox Priest Very Rev. Leonid Kishkovsky, it reveals church resistance, to which officialdom turned a deaf ear:*

'Grace to you and peace from God the Holy Trinity: Father, Son and Holy Spirit. As leaders from the World Council of Churches member communions in the United States we greet the delegates to the 9th Assembly with joy and gratitude for your partnership in the Gospel in the years since we were assembled in Harare. During those years you have been constant in your love for us. We remember in particular the ways you embraced us with compassion in the days following the terrorist attacks on September 11, 2001, and in the aftermath of Hurricane Katrina just months ago. Your pastoral words, your gifts, and your prayers sustained us, reminding us that we were not alone but were joined in the Body of Christ to a community of deep encouragement and consolation. Even now you have welcomed us at this Assembly with rich hospitality. Know that we are profoundly grateful.

Yet we acknowledge as well that we are citizens of a nation that has done much in these years to endanger the human family and to abuse the creation. Following the terrorist attacks you sent "living letters" inviting us into a deeper solidarity with those who suffer daily from violence around the world. But our country responded by seeking to reclaim a privileged and secure place in the world, raining down terror on the truly vulnerable among our global neighbours. Our leaders turned a deaf ear to the voices of church leaders throughout our nation and the world, entering into imperial projects that seek to dominate and control for the sake of our own national interests. Nations have been demonised and God has been enlisted in national agendas that are nothing short of idolatrous. We lament with special anguish the war in Iraq, launched in deception and violating global norms of justice and human rights. We mourn all who have died or been injured in this war; we acknowledge with shame abuses carried out in our name; we confess that we have failed to raise a prophetic voice loud enough and persistent enough to deter our leaders from this path of preemptive war. Lord, have mercy.

The rivers, oceans, lakes, rainforests, and wetlands that sustain us, even the air we breathe continue to be violated, and global warming goes unchecked while we allow God's creation to veer toward destruction. Yet our own country refuses to acknowledge its complicity and rejects multilateral agreements aimed at reversing disastrous trends. We consume without replenishing; we grasp finite resources as if they are private possessions; our uncontrolled appetites devour more and more of the earth's gifts. We confess that we have failed to raise a prophetic voice loud enough and persistent enough to call our nation to global responsibility for the creation, that we ourselves are complicit in a culture of consumption that diminishes the earth. Christ, have mercy.

The vast majority of the peoples of the earth live in crushing poverty. The starvation, the HIV/AIDS pandemic, the treatable diseases that go untreated indict us, revealing the grim features of global economic injustice we have too often failed to acknowledge or confront. Our nation enjoys enormous wealth, yet we cling to our possessions rather than share. We have failed to embody the covenant of life to which our God calls us; Hurricane Katrina revealed to the world those left behind in our own nation by the rupture of our social contract. As a nation we have refused to confront the racism that exists in our own communities and the racism that infects our policies around the world. We confess that we have failed to raise a prophetic voice loud enough and persistent enough to call our nation to seek just economic structures so that sharing by all will mean scarcity for none. In the face of the earth's poverty, our wealth condemns us. Lord, have mercy.

Sisters and brothers in the ecumenical community, we come to you in this Assembly grateful for hospitality we don't deserve, for companionship we haven't earned, for an embrace we don't merit. In the hope that is promised in Christ and thankful for people of faith in our own country who have sustained our yearning for peace, we come to you seeking to be partners in the search for unity and justice. From a place seduced by the lure of empire we come to you in penitence, eager for grace, grace sufficient to transform spirits grown weary from the violence, degradation, and poverty our nation has sown, grace sufficient to transform spirits grown heavy with guilt, grace sufficient to transform the world. Lord, have mercy. Christ, have mercy. Lord, have mercy. Amen.'

# ISRAEL'S ANTI-SEMITISM AND HOLOCAUST DENIAL

In the early 1970s an Israeli who had been brought up in North Africa and also had memories of Israel, leaned over a wall overlooking Jaffa/Joppa with Margaret and me, and mourned the change he had seen in fellow Israelis since his young days. Then Arabs and Jews had grown up as comrades, fellow Semites, enjoying one another's company. Israeli anti-Semitism had broken that bond. He groaned in heart-sorrow at that rupture in relationships. He did not call it apartheid, and the very idea is rejected in official quarters, but there is accuracy in the word. On one occasion, in work for the World Council of Churches when South Africa had still an apartheid government, I went straight from there to Israel. The sight of young Israelis, guns over their shoulders, sneering at Palestinians as if they were a lesser breed, confirmed the relevance of the word.

Since then the stealing of land to privilege one form of Semitism, the control of water, power, other resources for sustaining life to disadvantage the other form, and, in the end, a wall of division erected by Israel to separate the privileged from the dispossessed – how can that be described other than a form of anti-Semitism imposed to produce apartheid? 'An eye for an eye and a tooth for a tooth' has restriction in it as well as licence – only one eye for one eye, one tooth for one tooth. Israeli aggression is quite disproportionate. Its anti-Semitism is expressed in demanding thirty eyes for one eye, thirty teeth for one tooth. One of the reasons for bringing Saddam Hussein to book was his ignoring of UN resolutions. Israel's ignoring of UN resolutions is flagrant – yet they are not brought to book by the international community.

Israel is also in Holocaust denial, while accusing others of that position. We are meant to learn from past history, and not use wrongs done against us as a shield behind which we can work our national will, and get away with it as some kind of compensation for past suffering. One of the features of the Holocaust was the outrage of humiliating one people and exalting another over them. Israeli terror-ism has been expressed by invading Palestinian territory with the one-sided assault of heavy armour, killing relentlessly, bulldozing homes and leaving ruins. But oppression is also expressed in the humiliation imposed at checkpoints where Palestinians may be held up almost endlessly – as was the case with pass laws in South Africa. They are made subject, thus, to the will of the master race which seeks control of their destiny and robs them of human dignity and freedom.

Some Israelis look to the Bible to justify the occupation of territory. With the Holocaust in mind they should remember past history – how they were treated in Egypt, 'that slave-pen', as a lesser breed, and were brought out into freedom by God. That experience should burn itself into their memories so that they do not devalue other people as they were devalued in the Holocaust. Also they should remember that if they claim to be a nation favoured by God and heirs of the prom-ises, a warning is attached: 'You only have I known of all the families of the earth – therefore I will punish you for all your iniquities' (Amos 3.2). The warning is given that if, in turn, they become oppressors: 'I will raise up against you a nation,' says the Lord, the God of Hosts, 'and they shall oppress you (in turn) ...' (Amos 6.14). The Hebrew word for this kind of oppression is *lahats*, indicating a pitiless grinding down. In southern Spain I remember a painting of the Virgin Mary, putting her coat protectively around conquistadores as they went out to commit their holocaust of indigenous peoples. They also were acting in God's name!

It is time for Israel to reject the anti-Semitism which puts a wall of separation between them and fellow Semites; and to review the Holocaust as a warning against robbing others of their dignity and freedom.

It is time for the international community to recognise flagrant injustice and name it, and deal with it for what it is. When will we ever learn?

*Note:*
This reflection was written before the Israeli assault on Gaza at the end of 2008. Another Israeli then spoke out – deeply disturbed by the conduct of fellow Israelis. Avi Shlaim, Professor of International Relations at the University of Oxford, had, as he testifies in a *Guardian* article of 7th January, 2009, *'served loyally in the Israeli army in the mid-1960s and has never questioned the legitimacy of the state of Israel within its pre-1967 borders'.* He writes with horror of *'Israel's vicious assault on the people of Gaza'*, calling it part of *'one of the most prolonged and brutal military occupations of modern times'.* It is an example of *'a classic case of colonial exploitation in the post-colonial era'* where a people were subjected to *'deliberate de-development'*. This amounted to *'a fundamental rejection of the Palestinian national identity … it is a war between Israel and the Palestinian people, because the people had elected the party* [Hamas] *to power … Israel had a choice and it chose land over peace … Israel's entire record is one of unbridled and unremitting brutality towards the inhabitants of Gaza.'* [9]

# VILIFICATION AND REALITY: THE USA AND CUBA

*Written in 2008*

Vilification can stem from a justified judgement that some actions or persons exert evil influence. It can also stem from a reaction of hatred where actions or persons show up one's own priorities to disadvantage, and reveal an integrity which is baffling. Jesus warned followers about the latter. 'Blessed are you when people revile you and persecute you and utter all kinds of evil against you falsely on my account' (Matthew 5.11). The USA's vilification of Cuba falls into which category?

## Spiritual journeys

Among recent presidents of the US only Jimmy Carter has refrained from vilification. George W. Bush has shown an increased virulence in his antagonism. He presents himself as someone who has a hotline to God through which he gets his instructions in making large choices. He fails to submit judgements to fellow Christians, such as the US churches which opposed the Iraq War, or the international community which failed to give him the green light for it. Thus what can be attributed to God and to personal overconfidence and ambition was not sorted out: he pandered to right-wing Christian ideology whose adherents could be trusted to vote for him.

Fidel Castro reacted against the Church in his youth. It did little to oppose the corrupt administration of the dictator Batista. As a student he encountered Marxism, was attracted by the concern for justice, and became a Marxist. But he did not swallow Marxism whole. He kept an open mind. His relations with the Cuban communist party were fraught at times. He appreciated the link with the USSR which helped Cuba to establish a stable economy; but when in the missile crisis its representatives negotiated with Kennedy and Co. over his head, he looked more and more to the non-aligned countries until, in the early 1990s, Cuba became what in Latin American understanding is a 'lay state'; that is, one no longer holding to one ideology but allowing different religions and ideologies to make their own way according to their ability to attract adherents.

I just missed him when, in 1973, I stayed with the recently founded 'Christians for Socialism' in Chile. Fidel had been with them till a day or two previously. They had talked long into the night – Fidel was always a good listener, keen to hear any viewpoint so that full integrity was given to the mind of the person who held it – as is testified by his recent biographer, Ignacio Ramonet (*My Life*, Fidel Castro, Allen Lane, 2007). Castro concluded: 'With Christians such as you, Marxists such as I am can have not only tactical but strategic alliances.'

I was there when he spoke in the great square in Managua in 1980, when the first anniversary of the success of the revolution was celebrated. I stayed with Xabier Gorostiaga who was the equivalent of Chancellor of the Exchequer, responsible for economic development in the new Nicaragua. While I was there, a message came to Xabier, who was a Jesuit priest: could he please provide a list of theological books which Fidel should be reading. I was still there when the messenger returned the next day. Fidel had already read all these – what else should he be reading?

Fidel kept journeying in his thought. In the early 1990s he met with leaders of Protestant churches. A whole day of conversations was relayed on radio and TV to the Cuban people. Testimony is given to the fact that Fidel was a thoughtful, listening participant. Rev. Elmer Lavastida provided this account: '*The meeting with President Fidel Castro was April 4, 1990 in Havana. The President recognised that Protestants had been "discriminated" by the Revolution, and he promised to try to amend that error. He also stated that it would not be an easy task since many of the Party officials were educated in the Soviet Union and therefore had strong anti-religious feelings. But he gave his word to try to convince them of the new focus. This is what I remember of that historical meeting. And soon after, the effects were felt in different areas in which we had expressed complaint. For example, access of Christian youth to university careers and specific jobs, entrance of bibles and other literature to Cuba, possibility of receiving Christians from abroad and Cubans travelling to other countries (especially the USA and Europe), openness for the prayer cell movement in private homes, access to radio.*' When I spent six weeks as a visiting lecturer at Matanzas Theological Seminary, I sat beside a young man in the local Sunday services. One day he told me that he was a 'Marxist Christian'. For much of Cuba's history these two words would have been in contrast to one another, no longer so. He was clear that the noun 'Christian' was his life commitment. The adjective 'Marxist' was there to provide a justice edge to that direction of his life.

## Democracy

In Central America, especially in El Salvador, Guatemala and Nicaragua (where the destabilising and undermining of the marvellous people's revolution took priority) US policy was anti-democratic in a blatant and destructive way. Oppressive dictatorships were encouraged: in journeys in that region I heard the comment: 'We don't mind bastards being in charge, as long as they are our kind of bastards.' In El Salvador from 1978-81, 30,000 people were killed by right-wing death squads. In the 1980s more than 100,000 of the indigenous Mayan people were displaced to Mexico, as well as tens of thousands killed. In 1981, in Guatemala, an estimated 11,000 civilians were killed by death squads and soldiers.

If democracy was established, it was not approved unless it fitted in with US aspirations. When I returned from Chile in 1973, I wrote an article for *The Scotsman* saying that I could not see how Salvador Allende's democratically elected government could stand up to the destabilising activities of the CIA. In the same year Pinochet took over. In our day the refusal of recognition for the democratically elected Hamas in Palestine – the refusal to allow it to have a part in negotiations for a Middle East solution – affirms that it is democracy which is favourable to US aspirations which is wanted, not democracy as such.

Fidel Castro is accused of keeping in his own hands major decisions, controlling the life of Cuba. In conversation with Ignacio Ramonet, he called the regime 'democratic'. His remains the controlling voice. But he rightly argues that his is not a dictatorship in line with Latin American oppressive dictatorships. What oppressive dictatorship ever began its work with a literacy campaign? Illiteracy serves oppression; literacy gives voice to the disinherited.

US policies have made a tight regime necessary: During the literacy campaign (I have visited the Alphabetisation Centre in Havana), which reduced Cuban illiteracy to single figures, infiltrators picked off teachers who volunteered for assignments in remote areas. The BBC has noted 639 assassination attempts on Castro's life. When Ignacio Ramonet interviewed him, he was still sleeping in a different bed every night and having rare contacts with his brother, Raúl – in case one bomb should dispose of them both.

It was by chance that I was able to be present at an example of local democracy. In Matanzas I heard that a local election was to take place just below the grounds of the theological seminary. About 70 or 80 people assembled from the nearby streets. Gender sensitivity was shown – one part of the meeting was chaired by a man, the other part by a woman. A candidate was to be chosen to represent the area to serve in the body which had once been responsible for local defence – to keep alert to possible hostile infiltration of the area – and by that time was responsible for a variety of forms of social and neighbourly service. Those nominated had to be presented in terms of their good neighbourliness in their home area and their responsible conduct at work. Over, say, two hours, about three nominations took place, the nominators being questioned about their testimony, and discussion, relating local needs to the gifts of particular people, being widely engaged in. Over the period of the meeting, one could discern a movement of minds to one person, who eventually was elected.

## Priorities

George W. Bush unwittingly gave socialism a good name by dismissing any comprehensive healthcare proposals for the US as 'socialistic'.

Two Cubans who participated in the 2007 International School of Theology at Scottish Churches House, Miriam and Elmer (Elmer, a pastor and Miriam a pastor and a doctor), were interviewed by John McLaren, editor of the *Gargunnock News*. John reports of Elmer: *'He told me that, like any other country, Cuba has its pros and cons, but definite pros are its health service and its educational system, which is free to all, right through to, and including, university.'*

Vilification has been directed at both Nicaragua and Cuba because poor countries had the cheek to direct resources to much more positive and creative ends than the rich and powerful have been willing to address.

In Honduras I saw the broad roads – designed for military not agricultural vehicles – built with US money, which led right to the Nicaraguan border. Ronald Reagan's illegally-funded and sponsored Contra army targeted the hated schools and medical centres in Nicaragua – and announced to high heaven that the Nicaraguan Revolution could not be tolerated! Reagan put it forth that Nicaragua had become a military menace to the US. It was a menace all right – but a moral menace by its priorities.

The International Court of Justice found the US guilty of the destruction of Nicaragua's economy (which left that country with 60% unemployment). Disdain for international judgements was shown in that not one dollar was paid towards the reparations which the Court prescribed.

## Human rights

In 1998 there was a strong movement to get the UN to condemn Cuba for breaches of human rights. The UN rejected these attempts to get Cuba picked on.

When the sleazy, corrupt Batista dictatorship was overthrown, the Kennedy government, whose presidential predecessors had supported it, sponsored the Bay of Pigs invasion by Cuban exiles – just as Ronald Reagan had used the Contra army as cover for his assault on the Nicaraguan Revolution (Reagan called the Contras 'freedom fighters'!). In each case the determination shown was to control the life of the people of another country to fit in with US ambitions.

When George W. Bush became President he increased hostile pressure on Cuba, intensifying the illegal blockade which deprived Cuba not only of goods normally available internationally but of medical supplies, from lack of which many children died. In 2007, Dr Aleida Guevara, daughter of Che, a paediatrician, toured Britain and, wherever she could find them, picked up life-saving cancer drugs. On one visit to Cuba I was asked to take with me particular medicines. From the first morning after arrival these were eagerly and gratefully put to use. Later I was able to link up a Matanzas hospital with a UK medical missionary organisation, a device which allowed medicines readily available here and in the US to slip through the blockade.

During the Iraq War, illegal treatment of Iraqi combatants came to light, especially in Abu Ghraib. Guantánamo Bay suspects were not allowed normal rights of defence lawyers, limitation of time for interrogation, or due trial – this illustrates the way in which the Bush regime sat lightly to human rights. *The Guardian* of November 16th, 2007 reports the contents of a Pentagon manual leaked on the internet, giving main points concerning how prisoners are to be treated. The brushing aside of normal human rights comes through clearly. *The Guardian* provided a summary of the main points:

- *A behaviour management plan to 'enhance and exploit the disorientation and disorganisation felt by a newly-arrived detainee'.*

- *A reward system to encourage co-operation.*

- *Access to the Red Cross denied to some prisoners.*

- *Guards told the line to take with the media: 'We are making progress in the global war on terror through a concerted effort with coalition partners.'* [10]

## International responsibilities

Now that Latin American countries are rejecting neo-colonialism and taking their life into their own hands, we see no attempt to take developments in Cuba as a pattern to adopt. Fidel did not follow the Marxist-Leninist line by waiting for the working class to be conscientised and develop mass initiatives to overthrow Batista. He did not get behind the strikes Frank País led in 1958. He operated from the Sierra Maestra where volunteers in increasing numbers joined him; an urban basis was not considered to be essential.

The Cuban Revolution was an inspiration to many Latin American nations who resisted the attempted domination of global powers. Fidel's encouragement was 'Find your own way, drawing on indigenous resources.'

What is kept out of the headlines in the West, is Cuba's extraordinary service offered to the world to equip medical personnel and to bring appropriate aid swiftly and efficiently to areas of the world which have suffered major disasters.

a) With Venezuela, Cuba has committed itself to providing free medical training for 10,000 Latin Americans annually. An infrastructure to provide this training is being set up in Venezuela, which will share the responsibility with Cuban universities.[11] This contrasts with our own practice in Britain of enticing doctors and nurses, who have been equipped in poor countries at their country's expense, into our National Health Service.

b) In 1963, Cuba set up its first international medical brigade. '*In 1998 the Cuban government began to create the machinery to send large-scale medical assistance to poor populations affected by natural disasters. After Hurricanes George and Mitch blew through Central America and the Caribbean, [Cuba] offered its medical personnel as part of an integrated health programme. The Dominican Republic, Honduras, Guatemala, Nicaragua, Haiti and Belize all accepted this aid.*'[12]

The Kashmir earthquake struck in October 2005: '*On 15 October an advance party of 200 emergency doctors arrived from Cuba with several tonnes of equipment. A few days later, Havana sent the necessary materials to erect and equip 30 field hospitals in mountain areas, most of which had never been previously visited by a doctor … By the end of April 2006, shortly before their departure, the Cubans had treated 1.5 million patients, mostly women, and performed 13,000 surgical operations …*

'*Between 1963 and 2005 more than 100,000 [Cuban] doctors and health workers* intervened in 97 countries, mostly in Africa and Latin America. By March 2006, 25,000 Cuban professionals were working in 68 nations. This is more than even the World Health Organisation can deploy, while Médecins Sans Frontières sent only 2,040 doctors and nurses abroad in 2003, and 2,290 in 2004.

'The most seriously ill patients are often brought to Cuba for treatment. Over the decades these have included Vietnamese Kim Phuc, the little girl shown in the famous war photograph running naked along a road, her skin burned by US napalm. Cuba also took in some 19,000 adults and children from the three Soviet republics most affected by the Chernobyl nuclear accident of 1986.

[Cultural sensitivity is shown by the medical teams. In Pakistan, the women on the Cuban team], 'who represented 44% of some 3,000 medical staff sent ... dressed appropriately and wore headscarves. Goodwill was quickly established; many Pakistanis even allowed their wives and daughters to be treated by male doctors.'[13]

When, in August 2005, Hurricane Katrina devastated southern states in the US, the Governor of Louisiana, Kathleen Blanco, appealed to the international community for emergency medical aid. The Cuban government responded at once, offering Louisiana, Mississippi and Alabama a taskforce of 1,600 doctors equipped specially to deal with such catastrophes, the necessary equipment and 36 tonnes of medical supplies to arrive within 48 hours. But the Cuban offer, made both to authorities on the spot and directly to George W. Bush, did not even receive a reply from either. More than 1,800 people died for want of aid and treatment.[14]

Is it not a shame that a poor country like Cuba should undertake such an unselfish service to the world – in contrast to the policies of rich and powerful countries – and that this should move the rich and powerful to blanket out news of Cuba's initiatives? International responsibility of the kind described should be blazoned abroad as an incentive to others.

## Standing alone

We in Britain were given credit for standing alone against the Nazis when other European resistance collapsed.

Cuba should be given like credit.

In 1961 Cuba announced its intention to follow a Marxist-Leninist programme of economic development. In 1972 it became a full member of COMECON. The tie-up with the USSR proved beneficial, e.g. in buying up the sugar cane crop, producing economic progress. In 1991 came the collapse of the USSR. Fidel Castro was supposed to knuckle down to circumstance and take the capitalist road. But the Cuban response was otherwise. Sacrifices had to be made.

In 1972, as a member of the first official delegation from the World Council of Churches to visit Cuba, I had rejoiced to see Varadero – under Batista made the playground of gamblers, gangsters and the leisured class – swept clean of them and made available to basic workers who went there with their families as a reward for some outstanding service. The need for foreign currency returned the Varadero area (Fidel hoped temporarily) to tourists. I saw it in both the before and after versions, and thought the latter not nearly as damaged as the lovely coastal area had been in Batista's time – but I doubt whether it can ever return to the purpose of rewarding exceptional work on the part of basic workers, male and female, which gladdened my heart.

It was a difficult time when USSR finance was withdrawn. But Cuba retained its independence and pursued its different priorities.

Fidel considered the G8 summits to be an attempt by the powers-that-be to dominate the world to the disadvantage of poorer and weaker nations. He looked with hope to the new anti-globalisation forum which rejects G8 priorities and seeks, for instance, to introduce taxes on currency speculation. Fidel is, above everything else, a political animal, concerned to find just ways of working within nations and between nations.

## Is vilification justified?

When I returned from Cuba on the first occasion, my WCC report ended: 'There is something fundamentally right about Cuba.' When I returned from the first anniversary of the overthrow of the dictator Somoza in Nicaragua, my report ended: 'This is too good a revolution for it to be allowed to succeed.' Jesus was clear that pariah status may be wished on people without it being justified: 'Blessed are you when people revile you and persecute you and speak all kinds of evil against you falsely.' It is high time that the international community set its face against an illegal blockade of Cuba and all attempts to give it pariah status.

It may be suggested that Ignacio Ramonet's recent biography is much too uncritical of Fidel. He simply says, in rebuttal, that the international media have been so selective and biased in reporting the words and work of Castro that it was time to give Fidel opportunity to 'put the record straight' in his own words.

When I returned from my first visit to Cuba, I said to someone how marvellous it was to find people reappropriating their own history, instead of being tidied into the history of major competing powers. He answered, 'The record will be as biased as the colonialist one.' To this I replied, in turn, 'But you can get nearer the truth if you have two histories which have particular biases, than if you have only one.'

I myself have left out cases of Fidel's bad judgement, such as the military support of Ethiopia in its war against Eritrea (to fit in with Soviet policies). I have not made enough of the early failure to support Frank País and the urban revolutionaries. But I am not attempting a potted biography of Fidel Castro and the history of Cuba. I have been merely examining the possibility that attempts to defame Cuba and its leader are partly due to the threat of someone and some nation getting out of step with others; and, even more, that this taking of a different path presents national and international priorities which may put to shame those of the powerful.

## GETTING RID OF WAR

We must get rid of war – purge it from the face of the earth, recognise it as an abomination in God's sight, a desecration of God's creation and a thwarting of the purpose for which all life was brought into being. To have recourse to it is to allow that people made in God's likeness have a right to slay and mutilate others also made in God's image; often assuring themselves that they are doing this in God's name.

The testimony of those who survived the Battle of Iwo Jima speaks of human instincts being abandoned, human enemies treated as if they were like weeds to which weedkiller had to be applied to eradicate them at the roots. Only 212 of a Japanese garrison of 22,000 survived. US casualties were 6,891 killed and 18,700 wounded. US veterans testified how they felt the last grains of humanity draining from them, as they blasted away with bombs, guns, flame-throwers … War dehumanises. Enemies have to be caricatured – lest their real humanity be acknowledged and become an impediment to their brutal elimination. War encourages the conception that the world needs to be rid of such subhuman creatures.

Modern war produces a huge toll of civilian casualties. This is covered over where there is a refusal to give the total of civilian deaths and where these are shrugged off as merely 'collateral damage'. The urge to find inoffensive language to cover up the violating of human life is one of the 'war arts'! Lessons in dirty war tactics which kept in power oppressive US-supported dictatorships in Central America were shown up publicly. What was to be done? The programme was not much changed. The name was. The centre became the School of the Americas. What could sound more inoffensive?

Women are humiliated, violated by rape – the penetration of that secret core of being which should be yielded gladly and creatively only to the beloved. Forced entry demeans and disfigures both the victim and the base intruder.

In the bygoing, wildlife is decimated, fruitful land made desert. Legacies of landmines and scatter bombs are left to mutilate and kill. Resources are squandered which could feed and heal the world's population – amounting to a rape of the earth, its secret treasures looted; and a piling up of trouble for our children's children.

War feeds cravings for power. Combat to the death produces both fear and an adrenalin flow which puts combatants on a high. Where people's lives are dull or seemingly going nowhere it presents the lure of adventure, of life which has colour in it to combat drabness.

## What is to be done?

I am uneasy about the word 'non-violence'. For one thing, a positive approach to the elimination of war should be open to a positive name. For another, there are forms of violence which may be covered over, less easily recognised. The most violent words addressed to me in my life were in a note from George MacLeod which scarified me for adopting a multilateral approach to nuclear disarmament instead of his favoured unilateral one.

I prefer Gandhi's *satyagraha*. It comes from Sanskrit through Hindi, and brings together two words, *satya*, 'truth', and *graha*, 'grasping it to expose it'.

I have great sympathy for George MacLeod's position. He knew at first-hand the mud, the blood, the wanton destruction of life in the First World War, in which he was awarded the Military Cross. But in the early Iona Community I had at times to adopt the role of loyal opposition. When on one occasion I asked him if he had made up his mind whether to be a pacifist or a Christian, he shrugged off the question as if I were acting merely as a thorn in the flesh, as if my question were a non-question. I posed it quite sincerely.

Christianity requires two matters to be taken seriously and together. We have to search into the revelation of God's hand in history and, equally thoroughly, into the character of every tough situation faced; and bring the two into vivid, instructive relationship with one another. To have a position worked out in the abstract fails to produce both living theology and obedient action.

I considered pacifism to be a position taken up in the abstract without reference to the terms offered by situations to be dealt with, unrelated to gospel imperatives with which to address them. But I came across an instructive approach:

Graeme Brown, minister of the Church of Scotland, served in Nigeria at the time of the Biafran War. Every second day he had to take oversight of food supplies, delivered by air, to be distributed to feeding centres and refugee camps. The donor was Joint Church Aid. The food had to be delivered by lorry to the centres and camps. The lorries began to be held up and pirated by armed Biafran soldiers who had become detached from their units. Graeme's pacifism was put to the test. He decided to send the lorries under armed guards. To deliver the food safely might mean that some of those attempting theft were killed. But if the lorries did not reach the centres and camps, men, women and children would starve to death! He was clear that an absolute stance of pacifism had to be tested against reality. Some situations might require pacifism to be set aside even by those who would hold to it in many other situations.

In the Rwanda massacres, international military interventions could have saved life on a substantial scale.

I find the early Genesis stories instructive about our management of the earth.

They leave human beings with contrasting requirements: in chapter one 'fill the earth and subdue it' (Genesis 1.28), and in chapter two 'till and tend' the earth (Genesis 2.15). There is no escaping the word, translated from the Hebrew as 'subdue'. It means 'tread down', as a worker might with grapes in a winepress, as a people might be subdued (see Numbers 32, 22 and Joshua 18.1). God's way has a double aspect: 'filling and subduing' goes with 'tilling and tending'; 'hammer into shape' with 'love into shape'. I find this instructive. Preserving disappearing species can go with culling deer and elephants where food resources are inadequate or destructive tendencies develop. Till and subdue the earth can go together, both being an exercise of responsible stewardship. It may be that China, with its one-child policy, harsh as it may seem, has been acting morally in relation to its burgeoning population.

Monks on Iona may have offered no resistance to death-dealing Vikings, but governments of countries cannot responsibly act that way. There is a need for defence – if only to free from temptation rapacious countries which might take advantage of weak neighbours.

But how can the world be other than a field for the strongest? How can economically weak nations be protected from marauding forces? There is nothing for it but to look to internationally-effective forms of control. This includes intervention, military where necessary.

But UN forces have been found to collude with drug dealers and traffickers in all kinds of evil? They must be under closer control themselves. There is no alternative to having some instrument such as the UN and to continually vet and check it out so that it becomes more and more fit for purpose.

Finally, what is the objective to be? A world free of war? There is more to the Christian promise. The Greek word *eirene* indicates absence of war. The Hebrew word *shalom* indicates life in which all things work together for good: a rounded, satisfying way of living together in which every human being can contribute and receive in a fulfilling way. *Eirene* marks a stage. *Shalom* is echoed in Jesus' words: 'I have come that people might have life, and have it abundantly.' That is the goal. Zechariah, father of John the Baptist, made dumb until the birth of his son, was released into prophetic speech at the time of the child's naming. He saw, coming into being, a New Age which the child would herald, preparing the way for Christ's coming 'to give light to those who sit in darkness and in the shadow of death, to guide our feet into the way of peace'.

# THE TRINITY: A WAY OF EXERCISING POWER

Jesus said: 'Among the Gentiles (i.e. other nations) rulers lord it over their subjects; and those in authority are given the title Benefactor. Not so with you: on the contrary, the greatest among you must bear himself like the youngest, the one who rules like one who serves ... I am among you as a servant.'

This kind of power is presented as both sensitive to others and effective. Brute power is neither. The exercise of power in the Trinity not only illustrates such a way of power but becomes a sign for the way we should exercise power on earth.

The great graph of descent and ascent in Philippians 2 affirms Jesus' equal status with other members of the Trinity. He did not take advantage of that status and hold on to it but voluntarily gave it up, putting himself alongside the lowest in dignity of the human race as a slave or a 'nothing'. It was thus that he could fulfil the assignment committed to him as one made in the likeness of humankind: to bring health and salvation to humankind, and through them to the whole creation. He thus became the first-fruits of new life which death could not destroy – available for all creation wherever he is acknowledged and turned to. Once the assignment is completed he resumes his place in the fullness of the Godhead, bringing into it the humanity he had experienced. God is no stranger to what we have to go through in our earthly life. That experience is now in the heart of God.

In 1 Corinthians 15, Paul struggles to find words for this great mystery which has light and promise for us. The cry on the cross 'It is finished' might mean 'I've pulled it off: job done!' But yet Jesus Christ is, at that point, mastered by death, and belongs to the world of subjection in his human frailty. The resurrection reverses this. But does it reverse his status? The Philippians graph affirms that it does.

But all is not resolved at once. Jesus, risen, chooses Mary Magdalene as his herald of resurrection. In astonishment and delight she clings to him. He indicates that there is work still to do, disciples to persuade of this new reality, the resumption of his place in the Godhead, the sending of the Spirit – the time to cling is 'not yet'. When all is at last completed and everything is subject to him, 'then the Son himself will be subject in his turn to the One who subjected all things to him, so that God may be all in all' (Corinthians 15.28). This may seem to suggest that Jesus Christ remains subject to the Father. But his subjection is a reporting back, no more. When he has delivered the 'assignment completed' report he resumes his divine status. The Trinity is enriched by the accession of a truly human life.

The sign is given that to accept a low status may enhance, not diminish, the quality of the divine life. The affirmation is given that lives clothed with Christ, however low their earthly ranking, will belong in the heart of God when their earthly life is crowned.

The signal is given that any subjection of human being to human being must be merely functional, and willingly accepted to carry out a significant mission. As Jesus on earth had to wrestle in prayer to find and do the mind of the Father, so people on earth, given difficult assignments, may have to wrestle to respond to the will of the Father, who sees the whole picture more clearly. But that does not affect the final status of human beings made in the image of God. Mary, in her song, pictured it:

'He has brought down the powerful from their thrones and lifted up the lowly.'

Powerful people who are lowly are still accepted. But for the arrogant and cruel, Isaiah depicts a final comeuppance. His drama takes the form of the imagined death of one of the rulers of Babylon, who lord it in an arrogant and cruel way. He pictures such a one entering Sheol; the afterlife imaged as a ghostly, bloodless existence. Its inhabitants hear of his coming (Isaiah 14). They crowd to the entrance:

> *Sheol beneath is stirred up to meet you when you come;*
> *it rouses the shades to greet you, all who were leaders of the earth;*
> *it raises from their thrones all who were kings of the earth …*

They look up. Nothing!

They look down. A wizened walnut of a soul scrambles over the dividing line between life and death, this world and Sheol.

Their awed expectation turns to mocking laughter:

> *'Is this the man who made the earth to tremble, who shook kingdoms,*
> *who made the world a desert and overthrew its cities,*
> *who would not let its prisoners go home? …'*[15]

In contrast, Jesus illustrated the subjection which does not diminish final status but rather enhances it, by washing his disciples' feet. Jesus said to his disciples: 'I do not call you servants any longer … But I have called you friends.' The parable indicates the servant-way in which we should manage relationships on earth. The nuances remind us that this is a Trinitarian way.

Jesus presents himself as 'the Way'.

Whether or not he meant it intentionally, A.A. Milne reveals that this 'Way' is the way of reality. He does this in the poem 'The King's Breakfast':

> *'The King asked*
> *The Queen, and*
> *The Queen asked*
> *The Dairymaid:*
> *'Could we have some butter*
> *for the Royal slice of bread? …'*[16]

The dependency of the King on the Dairymaid is patent, though he tries to conceal it by using an intermediary to contact a mere subject, and by having the Queen insert the word 'Royal'. The Dairymaid knows that there is a more fundamental royal dependency – on the order of nature. If the *'cow … goes to bed'* the King is helpless to have even his most simple wish granted.

The Trinity made the world so that there is a mutual dependency which goes right down to bread and butter issues. To acknowledge this interdependency and to appreciate the gifts and contributions of others is to exercise true stewardship in creation after the manner of the Trinity.

# The church – as given to be, as found to be, and in the becoming

*As given to be:* The church as a body with Jesus Christ as the Head is one of the most telling ways of expressing what the church is given to be.

*The focus of this section is on church as 'body'. I start with a few cameos of Christ – sometimes poetic, sometimes humorous, sometimes both – to challenge misleading stereotypes, and later return to address the significance of Christ's uniqueness. The body, the blood, the means of the body's functioning provide the main material for this part.*

*There follows a consideration of the body's life in the world: evangelising not proselytising, rejecting fundamentalism, reaffirming the biblical understanding of sainthood.*

*The work of the Spirit is to make known Christ's mind and to guide the church to promote ways of life which lead to the establishment of God's Kingdom.*

*As found to be:* At times the shape of the church can become distorted from the basic type of image consistently given in the New Testament. Ecclesiastical authorities may shoulder aside the gifts of the Spirit-equipped community – whose resources need to be identified, matured and brought into play.*

*Hindrances to the full life of the church are examined:*

*Failure to follow through and equip the membership for its decisive ministry*
*Male domination*
*Protection of power positions*
*Power bids (resisted from within as well as outside the promoting body)*
*The relegation of ecumenical assignments to the background*

*Church in the becoming:* An attempt to discern what unity is present on the cards and what we aim for.*

*Church as given to be*

# CAMEOS OF CHRIST, THE HEAD

### The coming: Given in love

Given in love
before the morning stars
shouting for joy
announced a world was born:
                shorn
    … o …
equality's bright chain!;
chosen and sent
to be for our world spent.

Given,
exposed to slander, hate –
renounced
parachuting
angel hosts
importing aid:
       made
frail
as the least of all
stands in our place,
salvation for this race.

### The birth: Hush! Watch! Hear! (a carol)

Hush! Watch! Hear!
Something's in the air,
age-old hopes
seek fulfilment there:
Can it be – injustice,
twisting life awry,
will in death, defeated, lie?

Prick your ears –
may it be believed?
Suffering's
now a gift received!
May the prayers and patience,
all the tears and pain,
be converted to our gain?

Hold your breath –
dare we think it true
that our race
may be made anew:
twisted aspirations
turned from self and sin,
letting light and wholeness in?

Rub your eyes –
strange things are abroad,
see at work
our surprising God:
lays aside his glory
comes so weak and small
– doesn't look like God at all.

Hush! Watch! Hear!
Something's in the air,
age-old hopes
seek fulfilment there:
focus of all longings,
hope of hopeful strife,
is a tiny, human life![17]

## The wild card

*Translations of the gospels may do less than justice to some of the rough talk in them. In a carol, we are asked to sing 'the baby awakes, but little Lord Jesus no crying he makes'. ('Some hope!' says Mary in heaven.) Jesus bawled out the disciples when they kept the children from him (the Greek word* aganakteo *is stuffed with over-the-top irritation). He bawled out Peter when he tried to divert him from anticipating the Cross, calling him 'Satan'. Ironing out some rough stuff does a theological disservice. It reduces the reality of the Incarnation. Jesus was as human as they make them.*

Gentle Jesus, meek and mild,
cried the house down as a child.
Swaddling bands applied too tight
gave mum many a sleepless night.

Gentle Jesus, meek and mild,
grew an awkward God-willed child:
in the temple caused a fuss,
taught the teachers, missed the bus.

Gentle Jesus, meek and mild,
when a woman was defiled,
made accusers slink away
self-accused, that judgement day.

Gentle Jesus, meek and mild,
taught: God is not race-beguiled,
counts as equal, as God can,
woman, Jew, Samaritan.

Gentle Jesus, meek and mild,
where the money pots were piled
turned the tables, made a space,
there restored folk's praying place.

Gentle Jesus, meek and mild,
scourged, from angel power resiled;
treated as if human dross,
bowed his head, took up his cross.

Gentle Jesus, meek and mild,
trusted women (men were riled)
to announce his risen brief;
killing death, assuaging grief.

Gentle Jesus, on his throne,
will not stomach words alone:
'If your words with deeds don't gel
you're not mine: so go to Hell!'[18]

## At-one-ment

'For you,' he said, of life given.
'For you,' of blood shed.
How can this be?
How can one life,
one single life
conjoined to ours, stand in
for all humanity's capricious history,
eradicating foulness?

Yet he said 'for you',
for us, for us all, for all –
no need of it for himself:
for all.

Says St Paul: 'Put on the new humanity',
as lovers put on one another's life
– not taking over: honouring difference, affording space
and by the infusion of a new mind and spirit
enlarging life, becoming one: even so
in double harness, Christ and we become
destined to enter into the very being of God
completely, completely, utterly made one.
It's a promise.

Prayer

*You, through whom*
*all was created.*
*Who sloughed off privilege,*
*vulnerable before life's terms,*
*bearing the burden of bruised humanity*
*from the cross to the Father's throne,*
*discarding it there*
*for our at-one-ment:*
*we adore and bless you forever.*
*Amen*

## Jesus in nappies

*The reputation defended of one who deliberately made himself of no reputation.*

*Jerry Springer: the Opera* portrayed an adult Jesus in nappies. Some benighted Christian group sprang to the defence of Jesus, hounding performances to get them stopped (and at the same time providing free advertising for the play).

Is there a clearer way of saying that you are not seriously assaulting some character than by presenting him as an adult in nappies?

Some points are best made humorously by exaggerated contrast. Spike Milligan spiked sentimental songs such as 'I'm going home for Christmas' with his 'I'm walking backwards for Christmas across the Irish Sea'. We have been alerted to the menace of shark-infested custard. Eric Idle presented a bunch of crucified men singing 'Always look on the bright side of life', the hilarious contrast made all the more vivid by a gently galumphing tune.

Jesus adopted the same use of comic contrast when he depicted a camel trying to get through the eye of a needle.

Is *The Vicar of Dibley* a put-down of the church – or does it stem from an appreciation of odd and quirky features which can be exaggerated to produce laughter which has affection in it?

What about the raunchy elements? Consider bawdy bits in Shakespeare. Without these the range of human experience depicted would be diminished. We would

not laugh so much at our own natures, or reflect so much on their weaknesses –
to our instruction and fresh awareness of wrong behaviour to be put right.

In the end, who wants to put Jesus in nappies? Is it not the protesters?

Prayer

*Lord God, save us all from assaults on our intelligence*
*and sense of humour by po-faced Christians. So be it. Amen*

# THE BODY

The body is a mysterious and wonderful creation. I am speaking about the church
as Paul did.

Lungs and air were made for one another. Life is sustained when lungs and air
work together, especially when lungs are healthy and air is unpolluted. The in-
drawing and expelling of air in breathing oxygen cleanses the blood and removes
harmful carbon dioxide. The pulse sustains life, gives it quality.

The Hebrew word *ruach* is used for wind, spirit and breath – all meanings thought
of as means of preserving and enhancing the quality of life. In Jesus Christ's incarnation earthiness is reckoned to be a valid vehicle for divine activity. At the same
time, the struggle in Gethsemane can remind us that to do what God's Spirit
requires and what human flesh shrinks from because it is unwelcome or sacrifi-
cially demanding, means that a tug-of-war can go on between what is called biblically 'flesh' and 'spirit'.

Jesus, in his earthly life, had promised to send the Holy Spirit: 'When the Spirit of truth comes, he will guide you into all the truth … taking what is mine and making it known to you …' In his risen life he does this by breathing on the disciples: 'Jesus said again "Peace be with you! As the Father sent me, so I send you". Then he breathed on them, saying "Receive the Holy Spirit".'

Kissing may be thought of as the imparting of life-giving breath more than the savouring of lips. In 'The Lost Gospels', where Mary Magdalene is portrayed as a disciple so close to the risen Christ that Peter feels his position threatened, Jesus is depicted as kissing Mary quite frequently. Amorously? It is often assumed by scholars that he kissed her on the lips. But in the fragmented manuscripts which survive there is a gap. The kisses could have been on the cheek or on the forehead. If they were on the lips, the biblical notion of breath which imparts life must be taken into account. In the Gospel of Thomas, in saying 114, Peter confronts Jesus with 'Tell Mary to leave us – for women are not worthy of (spiritual) life.' Jesus tells Peter off, saying, 'I will make Mary a living spirit.' The imparting of Spirit could come from Jesus' breath.

If I were faced with the question 'If you had one piece of advice to give to following generations, what would it be?', I would have no hesitation: 'Lippen on the Holy Spirit' – trust, keep turning to and leaning on, staying in vivid relationship with, the Spirit. As the body needs air to survive so the church needs a constant, living relationship with the Spirit for it to be the body of Christ. For beyond all the laws, customs, duties which may be developed in the church is this necessity: to know the mind of Jesus Christ as conveyed by the Spirit of truth, and live out what is asked of us.

For this we need one another in order to discover what is really 'of the Spirit' instead of mere personal pretension dressed up as if it had a larger authority.

To live truly, attentively hearing and doing the will of God, the church must have recourse to the Holy Spirit continually.

# THE BLOOD

Life courses through the body as the blood is pumped out by the heart – 6,300 gallons of it every day through 96,000 kilometres of blood vessels! Every body is a universe. In our culture, the heart tends to be thought of as the seat of the emotions. In the Hebrew tradition, the heart is thought of more as the life-centre, including mind and judgement as well as emotions.

Blood poured out is a sign in the Old Testament of the longing for atonement. The letter to the Hebrews treats Jesus Christ's sacrifice as the one effective means of putting human beings right with God whom they have let down in so many ways. In the New Testament that act is more often referred to as 'the blood of Christ', rather than 'the death of Christ', to emphasise its atoning power.

The blood is pumped by the heart through the body's arteries and veins. It supplies cells with nutrients. It oxygenates, and removes waste products. The body is enabled to sort out, from intake through the mouth, what is to be used as good nourishment and what needs to be discarded. The church must be alert to make sure, as the body of Christ, that it is nourished by his sacrifice, and that it disciplines its way of life so that what nourishes it for mission and service in the world is accepted, and what opposes that way is got rid of. For its health the body must learn what builds it up and what would actually poison it. The church must live *semper reformanda*, constantly getting rid of what would actually threaten its life, so that it may remain a true sign that Jesus Christ who came from the Father to be the life of the world is manifest in the church.

To make clear to us what his life and work meant for our life in the world, Jesus left the scriptures, to be illuminated by the Holy Spirit. He also left a sacrament to bring this home as a reality of life which could run through our whole earthly way of living, as blood runs constantly through a body. He described this as his being one with the Father so that we might be included in the oneness, knit together, human and divine life intertwined. For this there had to be some kind of enlacing of his being with ours which does not usurp our own identity but enlarges and fulfils it. In Paul's epistles we find: Romans 13.14: 'put on the Lord Jesus Christ'. Galatians 13.27: 'As many of you as were baptised into Christ have clothed yourselves with Christ.' Ephesians 4.24: '… to clothe yourselves with the new self, created according to the likeness of God in true, right living and holiness'. Colossians 3.10: '… you have stripped off the old self with its practices, and have clothed yourselves with the new self, which is being renewed in knowledge according to the image of its Creator.' Colossians 3.5–25 spells out some aspects of the change. Baptism marks the change: the drowning away of an old life and rising to a new one.

The Lord's Supper or Eucharist provides means to receive Jesus Christ into our beings and our systems, 'putting him on' so that we manage daily life according to his mind more and more as faith matures. Bread and wine are used – no nectar of the gods but common fare within reach. Through Jesus Christ's provision this, blessed, becomes means of his life entering ours substantially. I see transubstantiation as one of the attempts to explain how real this entering in is; as the idea of being 'clothed upon' attempts also to picture a real change when Jesus Christ's being and ours are united. The Greek word *enduo* means literally to 'put on' or 'clothe'. It can also have the sense of one life being entwined with another, whether of a person or a community. Jesus Christ's life can be interlaced with human life, giving it freshness and new power.

I have had to overcome a reaction against the idea of drinking Christ's blood – expressed in his own words: 'Those who eat my flesh and drink my blood abide in me and I in them.' This, I believe, is partly explained by my own experience as a very young boy. My father was a butcher (or, more accurately, a flesher). He was blind and blindness and butchering do not go well together. But his brother took the front shop with its cutting-up work and dad did the manufacturing work in the back shop, helped before school by my brother and myself. A job I hated was stirring pails of half-congealed blood which were then mixed with other ingredients to produce black puddings. At that stage they were literally a bloody mess. I was in my mid-20s before I would get over my revulsion and eat one. I still avoid them if possible.

Yet, over years of presiding at Holy Communion, I have learned more and more to appreciate the prayer of invitation:

> 'Draw near with faith.
> Receive the body of our Lord Jesus Christ,
> which was given for you,
> and his blood which was shed for you;
> and feed on him in your hearts by faith
> with thanksgiving.'

Because nothing else conveys adequately the way in which, in the sacrament, Jesus Christ can enter into our very beings, substantially.

# THE HEAD

A body without a head is lifeless. The life of the church depends on adherence of the body to the Head as the life-giving, directing and guiding source for its whole existence. Jesus Christ is the Head of the church. In Romans 12.5ff and 1 Cor.12.12ff Paul spells this out.

The unique Headship of Jesus Christ is emphasised in the Bible in many ways. When he is depicted as the Good Shepherd, whose oversight of the flock is in order that they may 'go in and out and find pasture', I see a reluctance to call other leaders 'shepherds': under-shepherds, feeders of the flock, rather, represents our calling. The church must take care that, as the body, it finds life and direction in the Head. Every ecclesiastical authority has to bow to his authority and continually check its life in case it should be 'taking over', in clear or subtle ways trying to usurp that final authority. No one but the Head of the body can discern what the body should do and be. No other authority can represent the mind of God the Father and respond to it with full and true humanity. 'For we do not have a high priest who is unable to sympathise with our weaknesses, but we have one who in every respect has been tested as we are, yet without sin' (Heb 4.15). As is recorded in John 2.25, Jesus knew human nature through and through, experiencing it 'on the pulses', and not being taken in; yet he could claim to be one with God the Father – the Way, the Truth, the Life – and live that out. As Head of the church he has unmatched authority. As Colossians 1.15 says: *'He is the image of the invisible God, the firstborn of all creation. For in him all things in heaven and on earth were created, things visible and invisible, whether thrones or dominions or rulers or powers – all things have been created by him and for him. He himself is before all things and in him all things hold together. He is the Head of the body, the church. He is the beginning, the firstborn from the dead, so that he might come to have first place in everything. For in him all the fullness of God was pleased to dwell, and through him God was pleased to reconcile to himself all things whether on earth or in heaven, by making peace through the blood of his cross.'*

How can an earthly body of people, by means of a teaching authority (*magisterium*), do justice in witness to such a tremendous claim? How can it do so without acting as if it had a voice which should be unquestioned – that is, without some kind of takeover from Jesus Christ's overall authority?

Orthodox churches see Western churches as beguiled by earthly power. They believe they want position, clout – to be recognised (and sometimes feared) in and by the secular community. Jesus had warned against such power: 'The kings of the Gentiles lord it over others and those in authority are called benefactors. That is not to be your way' (Luke 22.25–27).

To represent Jesus Christ's way on earth the world is given the life of the body the church. To it is given the ministry which is in unity with His. But people arise who have special gifts and capacities to commend the Christian faith. In the letter to the Ephesians, they are listed thus: 'Some would be apostles, some prophets, some evangelists, some pastors and teachers.' But these are not to hold a dominating position. Their work is 'to equip the saints for the work of ministry, for building up the body of Christ …' How can responsibilities for teaching and leading others be exercised so that they play a servant, enabling role, mindful that Jesus said: 'You have one teacher and you are all students … you are not to be called instructor, for you have one instructor, the Messiah … The greatest among you must be your servant …' (Matthew 23.8,10,11)? Throughout history the church has had to struggle to get the balance right.

Dr Bernard Haring was a great moral theologian and a great human being. Before he died a few years ago he gave me clearance to use any of the material in the ecumenical thinking we had shared, which he had set down in conversations and letters. In one of these, dated June 6th, 1991, he speaks about the way in which the teaching authority (*magisterium*) is related to the one Teacher in his own Roman Catholic tradition.

I quote:

*'What about magisterium?*

*We all should never forget: there is but ONE Magister-Teacher, Jesus Christ.*

*What finally counts is who are the best learners, turning heart and mind to Christ, trusting the promptings of the Holy Spirit and sharing constantly with the best learners-disciples of Christ.*

*1. Among the learners-teachers first place is to be given to the saints, to the poor in the power of the Spirit, to the saints – prophets – witnesses, to those, trustworthy in their life and competent in their respective field – among them the theologians but not taken individually: separately, but within the Christian theological community.*

*2. The official magisterium*

*a) The Pope: decisive is: how good a learner is he? Listening to the Spirit, learning to know Christ and love with Christ, listening to the bishops and all those in pastoral care, listening to the saints, the prophets, the poor – paying the greatest possible attention to the saints and also to those competent in diverse fields, last but not least to the theological community, grasping thus ever more fully the* sensus fidei fidelium. *A decisive criterion is always how and how far the doctrines of a Pope and a Council receive a free consensus (the question of reception).*

*b) The Pope and the Council: Already Vatican I came to the conclusion that the teaching of the Pope is not haughty from above, but within the collegiality: this became more explicit through Vatican II.*

*c) The collegiality, Pope versus bishops, must not be severed from the solidarity and subsidiary principle regarding the whole people of God.*

*d) The role of the theologians as a community and the solidarity of their ministry in and for the Church:*

*There, too, the main question – how good learners are they, faced with Jesus Christ through the grace of the Spirit, faced with the humble ones, the prophetic women and men, etc?'*

# A MEANDER ROUND EVANGELISM AND PROSELYTISM

God interferes in human life very delicately and shows great restraint when pleaded with to intervene and magic away threats to human and other forms of existence. How is this for an example: God's beloved son is facing torture and death, and twelve legions of angels are confined to barracks! God wants fellow workers in the Kingdom to grow up. The attitude of the parent who says 'I won't let my child near water till she can swim' is not for Christians! Not only are human beings to be open to accident and human villainy; the natural order has been given a relative freedom and shakes its body into new positions through earthquakes and tsunamis. God stands aside when humanity is required to face dangers, to take risks and mature; and stands with us, unseen, suffering alongside. The promise is not a safety net but a presence, one which overcomes even death itself, as has been shown in Jesus Christ.

If, in distress, we call on the name of the Lord, we had better be clear what we are doing. The name represents the whole being. There is no good wanting a response from the aspect of God which would suit us: love, say, which rescues but does not question or criticise and judge. Rumpelstiltskin lost his power when his name was no longer his property. God's name will never become the property of another. We must be prepared for unexpected features, some of which will baffle and confound us. It was so with Job. He held to God in all the disasters which afflicted him. His wife, a fellow-sufferer, advised, 'Curse God and die.' Job would have none of it. 'Comforters', seeking to sustain him in his misfortunes, at first did a creative thing. They shared his grief and bewilderment in silence. But they then tried to fit him into their ideological boxes instead of taking on board the reality of his life and experience. Job says 'Up yours!', and demands to have it out with God directly. He is given his wish and finds he is a flyweight in the ring with the Heavyweight of heavyweights. The scene is marvellously comical. God's first blow floors him: 'Where were you when I laid the foundations of the earth?' Job's integrity has led him to this point of encounter. He then discovers that when you square up to the One who is the Name above all names, there is so much that you have not reckoned with that what is appropriate is awe. The 'beyond' in God, the unknown in God, means that encounter with God must be marked by awe (that is why worship gives life realism and proportion as nothing else can).

Evangelism demands awe; teachability as well as testimony. Proselytism assumes the role of Job's comforters, fitting people into ideological boxes.

Those who do not acknowledge the distance as well as the nearness of God are in danger of identifying their agendas with God's. Our security is in God's grip on us, not our grip on God. In the USA the 'moral majority' show a lack of biblical seriousness. Biblical words are treated as formulae which secure God's favour when built into conformist lifestyles. Jesus said that his words were 'spirit and life' (John 6.3), impossible to reduce to formulae. Paul warns against those who, demanding boxed certainties, interpret complex realities to fit in with their 'superior approach to life'. He urges Christians to be no longer 'infants … blown here and there by every wind of teaching' but … 'speaking the truth in love … to grow up into him who is the Head, that is Christ'.

In the Argentine the word *misión* is being replaced by the word *caminando*! *Misión* has a flavour of proselytism, with historical memories of conquistadores coming to convert people to Christianity with a Bible in one hand and a sword in the other. *Caminando*, 'walking together', provides a sign of genuine evangelism: the truth is sought in conversation, and instead of one being converted to the other's life-stance, both can be converted to a larger understanding of that reality which we call God. Should one influence the other to see things through his eyes, with his vision being unaffected by the other's perception, what has taken place is proselytism.

With very rare exceptions, to take over the life of another or of others, even at their request, would be a proselytising act. Instead of having indigenous resources and gifts brought into play to deal with the situation, the person or persons would be treated like an empty jug which needed to be filled with water provided from somewhere else (as Paulo Freire used to put it). No human being is like an empty jug. To be made in the image of God is to have qualities and gifts which can effectively be brought to bear on situations faced. The only exception which I have come across is where people have relevant gifts of which they are not aware or which they have been led to devalue. There it may be necessary to occupy their skin as far as possible – not to take over from them but to help them get a fuller appreciation of themselves. Whenever this happens, the initiator of the action withdraws, giving space for fresh-found resources to be brought into play by the person who has been unaware or unconvinced of these. Once the gifts are deployed that person can grow and mature. This approach is specially important with people who have been treated as failures and deprived of confidence by others or by their own diffidence. It can come home to them that they are made in the image of God and that they have a distinctive part to play in God's purpose for all life.

There is a heart-in-the-mouth element in taking this kind of approach. One builds up a store of experience over the years, out of which things 'new and old' can be drawn. There is a temptation to lay hands on some previous, successful way of dealing with a somewhat similar situation. It has always to be resisted. Every situation is unique. One has to stand, exposed and vulnerable, before the factors which come into the new challenge. One has to wrestle with the Holy Spirit to be shown a way. Previous experience may well play a part, and a creative one. But only provided each situation's uniqueness is taken on board. Evangelism always calls for Abrahamic risk, going out not knowing where that will lead. One lives with the concern: Will this prove to be a misguided reading of the situation, leading to a dead end, leaving people frustrated? Will they finish up being let down? The life of faith and life based on certainties are worlds apart.

When I was Dean and Head of the Department of Mission in Selly Oak Colleges, the staff team showed great sensitivity to the various needs of students. Any year we would have students from fifty or sixty countries and cultures. All had to have a reasonable grasp of the English language, but this one might have three degrees, the next one only primary school education. It was not some level of attainment which counted but the conviction of their church that they had potential for making a creative contribution on their return. The challenge was to meet them where they were and draw them on from there to a greater maturity in disciple-ship. The award of a certificate or diploma was related to the extent to which students had invested imagination and commitment for their equipping – not to some general level to be attained. (Contrast this with the 'high jump' approach of universities where the bar is the same height for those who start from solid academic ground and those who have to take off from the shifting sand of mini-mal educational opportunities.) Evangelism involves taking account of where and how people are placed and how they may grow from where they are in their own time and in their own authentic way. This results also in the evangeliser being evangelised, making growth in Christ.

I have found the marks of evangelism in funerals conducted – with so much thought and sensitivity – by Catherine Hepburn during her ministry in Gargun-nock. In preparation for the service she would sit down with the people most deeply attached to the deceased and listen to their thoughts and stories. From this listening she fashioned prayers and reflections which unveiled significant aspects of the life, helping people to hold it up to God. Afterwards she gave a copy of the service to the family. No other service would be the same because no other life would be the same. Thus she helped the local community to value and respect the life now removed from their midst; and crowned that life with loving remembrance. Since all kinds of people who were not kirk-greedy came to the kirk services, these were great evangelical occasions.

The heart of the difference of approach extends to our treatment of other living creatures. When my Uncle John was a boy he fell off the top of a loaded cart. He kept this from his father as he was not supposed to be on top. Bones became malformed in a small body, producing a hunchback. Donaldie was the farm's big Clydesdale. The love between that wee man and that vast horse as they worked together had to be seen to be believed. It seems to me that horse-whisperers have an 'evangelism' flair about their approach. The horse consents to the relationship, appreciates it. This is not so when horses are 'broken in'.

Yet soft approaches are not always called for. When Margaret and I went to the parish of Rosyth it was in a situation of breakdown. As things got worse, competent people had given up on assignments and kindly volunteers had taken over to keep the show on the road. It was soon clear to me, as it had been clear to others, that resignations in all the major offices were called for to allow the church to get new life. I got these! It was a tough job to tackle. But once the situation was hammered into shape a fresh start could be made.

On a large scale there is a 'proselytism' where a powerful nation bends another nation to its will, imposing its values as if they were universal, brushing aside realities in the other which could enlarge its own life, if only it were teachable. There is, in contrast, an 'evangelism' flavour where nations, in dialogue, negotiate with respect for one another – where the historic features and pressures with which each has to reckon and where different cultural and religious differences are taken into account. The positive possibilities for peaceful resolution can be explored thoroughly without a critical edge being lost. Nations have to learn to live with differences. Subjugation spells impoverishment for the victor as well as for the vanquished. It is an advance in international peacemaking where a body such as the UN can provide means for negotiation and for holding in check aggressive powers.

Proselytism allocates to the proselytiser a superior position: success comes when the one addressed accepts the other's way of seeing things. When Pope Shenouda of the Coptic Church invited me to meet with him, he asked what I would like to be the focus of our conversation. I suggested 'mission'. 'In that case,' he said, 'put away your tape recorder. Anything I say, however carefully handled, may get back to Egypt and be distorted to make me out to be a proselytiser. I do not want the trusting relationship I have with the Muslims to be put under threat.' Later in the conversation he said to me: 'Evangelism can be compared to a seed which needs outside influences – earth, sun, rain – to enable it to stir into life. But it must then grow *as itself*.' Perceptive!

# FUNDAMENTALISM

The faith for which the church stands is distorted wherever a fundamentalist approach is adopted.

A basis was laid in tracts published in the USA, the first of which was *The Fundamentals*, published in 1909. An honourable intention lay behind the enterprise: to identify the essential elements which characterise Christian faith. But those who undertook it brought to the task conservative assumptions which led them to fasten on dogmas whose fundamental assertions can well be disputed. One emphasis is the inerrancy of scripture. Throughout history evidences are discovered which test sources and challenge contemporary interpretations of scripture. (For instance Mark's Gospel depends directly on the witness of Peter. What are called 'The Lost Gospels' throw fresh light on Peter's role.) The fundamentalist discounting of biblical-historical criticism meant rejection of a valid tool to get to the truth. Reliance was placed, instead, on a dogmatic position, impervious to awkward questioning. The fundamentalist position professes to honour God, whereas actually it represents a human search for a security which neither human beings nor God can gainsay. Jesus said it is the Spirit who must be turned to to lead us to the truth. The Spirit does not produce iron-clad forms for understanding God's will and living God's way which guarantee divine approval at the end of the day. We are to live by faith, not sight.

Jesus encountered an earlier form of fundamentalism in the manner in which the Mosaic law was addressed in his day. He scarified scribes and Pharisees for concentrating on the letter of the law, not its heart: 'For you tithe mint, dill and cumin, and have neglected the weightier matters of the law: justice and mercy and faith' (Matthew 23.23). When they relied on their descent from Abraham, to justify their behaviour, John the Baptist reminded Pharisees and Sadducees that God was not to be tied to tradition: 'I tell you, God is able from these stones to raise up children to Abraham' (Matthew 3.9) – note, not just children fashioned from stones but children of the promised line. There is no conveyor belt of conduct which will lead to God: faith is called for, with all the risks entailed.

Jimmy Carter in his book *Faith and Freedom* indicates the damage to Christian faith produced by right-wing fundamentalists in the US. Their way of life is marked by 'rigidity, domination and exclusion', he declares.

*Rigidity*: People are required to adhere to a defined pattern of thought and conduct designed to win God's favour. In reality this is a false way of seeking security for oneself, masquerading as a true way of glorifying God.

*Domination*: 'You must leave your ground and come on to our ground to be saved' is the form of invitation given by fundamentalists. This way is not open to teachability before other approaches in the community of faith.

*Exclusion*: Those who do not accept their position are shut out. A partition tightens around those who adopt a fundamentalist stance, blocking others out.

Those who are attracted to the Christian faith may be put off if rigidity, domination and exclusion mark those who profess that faith.

# SAINTS MADE/UNMADE

We have replaced the New Testament understanding of saints with a much more restricted use of the term, to the detriment of the communal vision; compare this with Paul's salutation to the Philippians: 'All the saints greet you, especially those of Caesar's household.'

'Saints' are 'those being sanctified', that is, growing more and more like Jesus Christ in their character as the years go by. They are a ragtag and bobtail army, who do not live on a level of perfection unattained by others; rather who may falter in faith and fail, letting God and the cause down – but get the grace to pick themselves up, dust themselves down and soldier on. They live not by immaculate attainment, but by dependence on God's forgiveness.

We have reduced the understanding of saints by focussing on prominent achievers. Some of these may be humble and obscure. But they have been extracted from the ruck, even their humility highlighted as a cause of merit, given headlines instead of a quiet obituary notice; their lives put in contrast with others who live faithfully: as if they were models to be emulated rather than to be treated just as companions on the road, fellow pilgrims in faith.

A flawed understanding of sainthood is reinforced when any church takes upon itself, at an official level, the designation of saints. It is the Holy Spirit who identifies saints, and they are a motley company! When a church takes on the job, you can be sure of two results: Those who are dead and dusted will have those characteristics emphasised which are not threatening to the church of the day, or will have sharp and challenging points filed and blunted. Too many will accord with ecclesiastical stereotypes, especially clergy and clergy-like examples. The normal processes of securing evidence for appointing saints can be interfered with. Pope John Paul II initiated fast-tracking in order to get Mother Teresa into that bracket. Her work was saintly. But she was also a religious conformist, never challenging Vatican decisions. She fitted into a churchly conception of sainthood. She lacked one of the saving qualities of the company of saints – a realisation that the church is an inadequate instrument for bodying out the Kingdom, and needs to be continually brought up sharp where it fails to do so, so that it may mend its ways.

Pope Benedict XVI has adopted this change in appointing, seeking that Pope John Paul II be fast-tracked to sainthood – and, by this, setting in place a papal stereotype which suits his own mind (and prepares for his own elevation in due time).

All this obscures the gospel understanding. Where are the single parents who bring up children not brilliantly but reasonably well? Where are those who, like ploughmen and potters in an earlier day, 'are not remarkable for their ... grasp of the law ... or for culture ... but give solidity to the created world' – by their daily work of sustaining it? (Ecclesiasticus 38). Where are those who simply act as neighbours, giving food to the hungry, drink to the thirsty, hospitality to strangers; who clothe the naked, visit the sick and prisoners? They do not feature in any calendar of saints. But they are all there, every one of them whether well known or little known, 'when the saints go marching in'. For they belong to the gospel understanding of sainthood. Is the official making of saints a way to try to unmake God's saints?

Why should so many be disinherited by this attempt of the church to expropriate the identification of saints, making an industry of it which diverts people from genuine Kingdom assignments?

Fortunately, people are wiser. When the official authorities get it wrong and become strangers to the gospel intention, Jesus himself said 'they do not recognise the voice of strangers'.

Yet it is a pity if churches focus on special types of Christians instead of seeing that all are 'called to be saints' in a community of love and service. I thought I would try to set the record straight with a hymn:

## The saints of God

*The saints of God are down our street*
*and round God's throne of light.*
*There's some with formidable minds*
*and some just live aright;*
*together in God's family*
*their different gifts unite.*

*They serve at checkouts, empty bins*
*and teach and make and mend;*
*they feed the hungry back from school,*
*the victimised defend;*
*to voiceless folk they lend an ear*
*and immigrants befriend.*

*Their efforts gain no accolades,*
*they simply earn that grace*
*which heals the world of many sores,*
*renews its battered face –*
*through such – who live and love and care*
*in their own time and place.*

*When death comes knocking at their door*
*they'll look at Christ askance –*
*how could such ordinary lives*
*his Kingdom ends advance?*
*But Christ will say, 'It's party time –*
*come, friends, and join the dance.'*

*Church as found to be*

# CHURCH AS FOUND TO BE: SHAPE, RESOURCES, HINDRANCES

A football commentator might say of a defeated team that the problem had been 'it lost its shape'. People played haphazardly instead of fulfilling assigned roles. Keeping shape gives coherence, allows resources to be deployed to the greatest effect.

According to the biblical witness the church has a basic shape. It agrees with Jesus' saying in Matthew 23.8: 'You have one Master, the Christ, and you are all brothers and sisters.' There must always be a concern that there be one Head, Jesus Christ. This is expressed in other related biblical images: Householder and household, God and God's people; the Temple as the place of worship is depicted not as a building but as a community, a spiritual house of living stones with Jesus Christ as the foundation on which everything else depends. In images taken from nature (vine and olive tree), Jesus is the stem on which the branches depend for life and for fruiting. The image of final consummated relationship is of Bridegroom and Bride. Peter in his first epistle tumbles over himself in describing a body of people who have a unity with one another and unity with the Head (Peter 2.5, 9–10): 'an elect race, a royal priesthood, a holy nation, a people of possession, the people of God'.

Paul described the way in which the body gets its shape. Joints, organs, muscles have different parts to play in building it up for its life of love and service in the world. No part is given a higher rating than another, 'that there might be no division in the body but that all parts might feel the same concern for one another'.

The church must appear to many today to have lost its shape. Instead of looking like a body as set out in the scriptures – a unity with the different parts working in harmony to build it up – it must look more like a modified Michelin Man in three layers:

a) One which has higher visibility and seeks to give the church direction, mainly comprising those of us who are clergy.

b) One which comprises 'full-time religious' such as monks, nuns, charismatic leaders – who can be thought of as a spiritual elite. An exposure of this kind of thinking is found wherever the word 'vocation' is restricted to layers/categories a) and b), as if Jesus' work as a carpenter was not a genuine vocation. The idea that some such members of the church can be thought of as specially religious was one which Jesus contradicted not only by words but by associating with 'publicans and sinners'. Sinners could be a classification indicating both those under justifiable moral judgement and those who did not observe all the intricate rules and regulations of the religious industry of the time: For one thing, they had to earn their bread and look after families, which took up most of their day. For another, they were confronted with requirements which did not make sense.

> *The word sinner* (hamartolos) *had a double significance. It did mean a man who broke the moral law; but it also meant a man who did not observe the*

*scribal law. The man who committed adultery and the man who ate pork were both sinners; the man who was guilty of theft and murder and the man who did not wash his hands the required number of times and in the required way before he ate were both sinners.[19]*

It is not that, customarily, those who are in category b) look for higher status, it is simply that any such hierarchical thinking must be combated to prevent a distorted idea of church.

c)  A third layer is called 'laity', making it into a category or layer, whereas the word *laos* in the New Testament describes all God's people. All members of the church are 'laity', with different assignments.

The Vatican II Council, conscious that its Vatican I predecessor had put too much weight on hierarchy, draws its definition of church from the first letter of Peter to the 'people of God', in Greek, the *laos* of God. It is to the *laos* that the ministry on earth is committed, to act in unity with Jesus Christ's High Priesthood, the *laos* in its totality. Every other ministry's work is to enable and resource that definitive ministry.

Bishop Lesslie Newbigin and I both moved membership to 'the church of the land', the United Reformed Church, when we went to Selly Oak, Birmingham. On one occasion we were asked to go to the headquarters in London for consultation. We found that the question to be debated was whether an auxiliary ministry should be instituted. We both burst out making the same point, 'But you have that already. That is what we are. We are auxiliary to the ministry of the church.'

In no way may the Headship of Jesus Christ be impaired.

What worried Paul about the situation in Corinth? Churches seemed to be divided in their allegiance: 'I am for Paul', 'I am for Apollos', 'I am for Cephas', 'I am for Christ'. Horrified, he asks, 'Is Christ divided? Was Paul crucified for you? Were you baptised in the name of Paul?' He goes on to recognise that different agents might well be acknowledged to be influential, as long as they are not considered rivals to Jesus Christ's Headship: 'I planted the seed, Apollos watered it, but God made it grow. We are fellow workers in God's service.'

It is significant that the three agents mentioned (Paul, Apollos, Peter) represent different stages in the development of the church. Peter was there from the beginning, one of the original apostolic band. He laid down the qualification to belong to that company in Acts 1.21,22: to have accompanied Jesus Christ in the course of his earthly ministry and to have met him in his risen life.

In our own day we see small 'house church' communities coming into being all over the world, and new leadership being thrown up, often not individual but communal in character – this person emerging with gifts to meet a particular situation and giving way to that one with different gifts to meet some different trial or opportunity. The body of the church can be built up for selfless service in the world as all the different parts contribute to the whole.

For the church to adopt a modified Michelin Man shape frustrates the task of equipping the body with gifts for its life, in major ways.

When, in relation to some public issues, the mind of the church is asked for, it is those from the top layer who are turned to, not those in the body who have a committed faith and the appropriate competences. Leadership in the church should imply, for one important thing, knowing who in the community can provide appropriate resources which can be brought to bear, and affording them place and voice.

Pope Paul VI (an underestimated Pope?) was aware of this reality. In preparation for the encyclical *Humanae Vitae* he established an advisory committee consisting of people with a range of experience, married and otherwise. This enriched the encyclical. But he himself went against the advice of that group, which had the required competences, by rejecting the responsible use of contraceptives. The final word should have been with the people of experience, not a celibate (celibates are also sexual beings – but I would not give a job to a plumber who had learned his trade only in a classroom).

## Hindrances

### a) Failure to follow through: Equipping the saints

This failure has been authoritatively recognised. One very constructive informal initiative ran alongside the life of the Vatican II Council. Rosemary Goldie, an Australian nun, was Executive Secretary of COPECIAL, the Permanent Committee for International Congresses of the Lay Apostolate. I was told that when she and Pope John XXIII got their heads together it was impossible to identify which one had originally thought up some possible line of action which both advocated. However it was that this project took wings, the result was that the World Council of Churches was invited to provide fifteen officially appointed Orthodox, Reformed and Lutheran representatives to meet with fifteen Roman Catholics, appointed through COPECIAL: to consult informally together on 'The Church in the Modern World'. The first meeting took place in January 1964 before the fourth and final meeting of the Vatican II Council. Its concern was 'The Respective Roles of the Laity and the Specially Ordained Ministry within the People of God'. It produced profound listening and sharing of faith perceptions. Each day started with sacramental worship – a Mass, an Orthodox Eucharist and a Church of Scotland communion service (which I conducted).

The next consultation, in 1965, was on 'The Formation of the Laity'. I co-chaired the three days, along with the Executive Director of the National Council of Catholic Men (USA). Participants, building on the Vatican II Council's affirmation that the church is 'the people of God' and that theirs is the definitive ministry which accompanies Jesus' High Priesthood, turned their attention to the way in which all the members of the church might be equipped to develop the many gifts of the Spirit so that these are built effectively into the common ministry. We (all thirty) came to an unanimous mind on the matter, which we thought should be presented as a challenge to the concerned churches:

> *Resolution adopted by plenary session:*
>
> *We, the members of the informal consultation called jointly by COPECIAL and the Department on the Laity of the World Council of Churches, unanimously agree*
>
> 1) *that the training of the laity should be considered as a priority in the policy, programme and allocation of finance of the churches represented, and*
>
> 2) *that all suitable opportunities should be taken by the Roman Catholic, Orthodox and Protestant Churches to co-operate together in this field of lay training, and to share insights, personnel, facilities and other resources of movements and centres.*

Proceedings of this ecumenical consultation (September 7th–10th, 1965) are published in the book *Laity Formation*, a joint publication of COPECIAL and the Department on the Laity of the World Council of Churches. Note that this editorial point is made: *This material is not meant, however, to remain a monument to three days packed with prayer in common, hard work, some fun and much fellowship. It is intended essentially as a stimulus and starting point for further prayer and reflection and even for appropriate action – according to the needs and the possibilities of each concrete situation.*

This recommendation was ignored, and continues to be largely ignored.

## The biblical basis

Paul puts it plainly. Those who are given special assignment in the church are allocated special responsibilities. They are not given special status. Jesus himself sums it up: 'One is your Master, the Christ – you are all brothers and sisters.' In Ephesians 4.11 Paul declared of Christ: 'It is he who has given some to be apostles, some prophets, some evangelists, some pastors and teachers *to equip the saints for the work of ministry ...*' The definitive ministry is that of the people of God. Those who have special assignments are auxiliaries to help this to happen. Jesus quoted his own servant status as an example and was quite blunt about what this meant for all his followers: 'The greatest among you must bear himself like the youngest, the one who rules like the one who serves' (Luke 22.26).

There were no successors to the original band of 12 disciples. What happened was that small companies of Christians came into being and threw up, from within their ranks, those who were given special assignments to equip God's people for their ministry. It was Paul, originally an outsider, and Barnabas who, in Antioch, 'appointed elders for them in each church' (in those days these would be house churches). Paul's concern that there be a good leadership team in each church is shown in his letter to Titus. So the promise of Jesus to 'the apostles whom he had chosen' that they would be 'baptised with the Holy Spirit' and 'be my witnesses in Jerusalem, in all Judaea and Samaria, and to the ends of the earth' was realised in a sprout of churches here, there and everywhere. At Pentecost all the people were given gifts by the Holy Spirit so that they might be equipped for a share in the work of ministry in and to the world. The work which went on to express and mature these gifts is given expression in 1 Corinthians 14. There participants, instead of leaving every act of worship in the hands of a priest or pastor, build up the worship at one and the same time, using their gifts and maturing them by disciplined use.

The word 'evangelist' need not indicate an assignment which lasts a lifetime. There may be a variety of jobs in one lifetime. Sometimes the needle gets stuck in one groove when it would be better to move on. If Billy Graham had come down from his mountain to get more in touch with the world's people and the challenges of history he might have confronted Richard Nixon on the invasion of Cambodia and Park of Korea on his seamy regime, instead of simply accepting the red carpet treatment.

One could be called to be an apostle in some unevangelised area of the world or unevangelised area of thought and expertise; do evangelising work there for a period; be prophetic about the conditions of the people and what that might lead to: and then, when the situation was more settled, end life as a pastor and teacher. Availability to God may be expressed in different forms in one life.

Modern translations of the Bible give the true meaning of ordination. It simply means appointment. Any idea that it introduces some special character into those set apart amounts to a clergy power-bid and has no biblical warrant. The most impressive declaration of the role of clergy I have come across was in a Guatemalan church of native Indians. It was wordless. The priest entered with his clerical robes over his arm, and put them on in front of the congregation. He conducted a participant service. Before leaving he took off his robes and went out with them over his arm, resuming his place as an ordinary member of the congregation, being ministered to as well as ministering to others.

## The maturing of gifts (Scotland and Nicaragua)

The resources of the church need to be brought into play and matured.

In the twelve years that Margaret and I served in Rosyth Parish Church the identifying and maturing of gifts played a prominent part. From the beginning, members learned to be praying people by contributing in the Healing gathering after the evening service. Then it came to the point that, if I had to be elsewhere of a Sunday, I could detail three volunteer elders to take each service, one responsible for the general structure, one for the prayers, one for the sermon and children's talk. Working together gave them confidence and developed a common mind. I could also at times leave the sermon to the congregation, either when meeting in groups of five or six in the hall and sharing insights, or in church in a communal exercise (one of the biggest risks I have taken in my life). But this was only possible after years of equipping the members through relating the Bible to dockyard and world issues, the elders having an hour of Bible searching to start every session meeting, and the Women's Guild and Women's Fellowship and the Youth organisations and Sunday School having an equivalent biblical basis for their life and work. Also every year, in Elders' District Socials, members in three districts at a time looked at the way they were fulfilling caring responsibilities in their patch and in the world. In this whole process one could see different gifts and callings emerging.

The responsibility of those of us who are ordained is not to be ourselves frontmen and frontwomen but to enable the ministry of the people: note, 'some to be apostles, some prophets, some evangelists, some pastors and teachers *to equip the saints* (i.e. the punters) for the work of ministry, for building up the body of Christ ...'

To ask top-brass ecclesiastics to give the mind of the church on particular issues is like entrusting all kinds of challenges to a mechanic who has a favourite spanner he will pull out to tackle every kind of problem. The church is like a toolbox where the right instruments (embracing faith and competence) have to be sought out and brought to bear.

One of the most rewarding things Margaret and I ever heard came from my successor, Ian Cowie, speaking to the Iona Community after he had taken stock of the Rosyth situation as he found it. In the six months' vacancy, yes, there was an interim moderator; but the ministry of the church continued without let or hindrance in the hands of gifted people, he testified.

All over the world Christians in small communities exercise Spirit gifts and mature them. A bus driver told me that he had been a churchgoer but had given it up. He insisted, 'I didna gie up on God, just on the Kirk!' I asked why. He replied, 'I just asked myself: "What dae I do?" and realised that I just sit. What's the good o' goin' there and just sitten? So I gaen up on it.' The gifts of people need to be identified and matured in the *practice* of worship and service.

Here is one example from my travels for the WCC: I go to the Iglesia La Merced in Nicaragua. The priest has a hand-held microphone. At both times of prayer he asks the congregation who or what to pray for. They mention persons or causes – or say 'Gimme the mike' and offer prayer themselves. At sermon time he takes four or five minutes to start exposition of a passage of scripture – then the microphone is handed round and the congregation build up the rest of the sermon. Superficial scrape-off-the-head stuff? Anything but. The congregation consisted of members of seven small Christian communities, who had met separately during the week, shared knowledge of who and what should be prayed for, reflected deeply on the theme and scriptural text for the week, and came together to share in worship. It happened this way in the early church. The habitual way of worship is set out in 1 Corinthians 14.26–38.

Scotland offers an alternative of substance to top-down approaches. Action of Churches Together in Scotland draws together under one roof in Alloa initiatives of different churches; and Scottish Churches House in Dunblane, a house of the churches together, can uniquely provide for substantive thought on particular issues, drawing on apposite church and world resources.

## Hindrances

### b) Male domination: endemic male assertiveness

A programme on BBC 4 on 'The Lost Gospels' – those which did not get into the New Testament – pulled me up sharp. I realised I had read them breaking a major rule of scholarship: I had scanned them through the spectacles of those who had dismissed them as unauthentic, erroneous or even heretical. A text which is worth attention needs to be allowed freedom to make its own impact. So I read them again, hearing what they had to say. What they had to say not only made sense in itself, but made sense of some awkward points of the scriptures as we have them now; and suggested that male determination to dominate the record and the tradition had early overcome the sign which Jesus gave by his conduct towards women, that they and men were equally made in God's image.

I can get the feeling that behind some scriptural texts something is going on which is not surfacing. It may be months, years before I can put my finger on what causes the sense of disturbance and get some clue to what may be at the root of it and what further light might be shed, breaking open familiar understandings. Then that light can be offered – for consideration only. Evidences exist in hints, nuances of narrative.

The focus came to light on that extraordinary character, Peter. Many blue moons ago, at a theological conference held near Crewe, John Henson, author of *Bad Acts of the Apostles*, and I shared thoughts about Cephas, the Rock, and agreed that he might at times justify the designation 'Rocky'. I distinguish an instability, particularly from the time that Jesus sets his face to go to Jerusalem. I think it may be a question of status, Peter's idea of the proper status of a Messiah and of himself as the leader of the Messianic group.

The Gospel of Mark is particularly associated with Peter and must have appeared soon after his martyrdom in 64 AD. Somewhere around 140 AD Papias notes: *'Mark, having become the interpreter of Peter, wrote down accurately everything that he remembered, without, however, recalling in order what was either said or done by Christ. For neither did he hear the Lord, nor did he follow him; but afterwards, as I said, followed Peter … for he made it his care not to omit anything that he heard, or to set down any false statement thereon.'* Around 200 AD Irenaeus adds that Peter's friends urged Mark to make a written record of the teaching which had been made known to him orally; and Clement of Alexandria confirms that this was done before Peter's death. The authenticity of Peter's testimony is undisputed. But I wonder whether a chastened Peter, looking back, was honest about defects in his own character.

Just over a third of Mark's Gospel is occupied by the last week of Jesus' ministry. Here two sides of Peter's character come out clearly. He seeks assurance: 'Look, we have left everything and followed you.' And gets the answer that, for such, the harvest in this life will be a hundredfold (with persecutions), followed by eternal life in the age to come. Yet Jesus adds a warning: 'Many who are first will be last and the last will be first' – as if to correct any impression that they could think more highly of themselves than others. Their status was to be like their Master's – servant status (Luke 22.24–27). Mark puts together (in chapter 8) Peter's confession that Jesus is the promised Christ (Anointed One, the Messiah) with Peter's act of rebuking Jesus when he openly anticipates and teaches his suffering and death. It may be that these came closely together in time. But if not they indicate that Mark associates them as two sides of tension building up as things come to a head in Jerusalem.

My concern rests on the use of one Greek word, *proslambano*. Consider the emphasis the word implies. The sense of the word is of the knowledgeable enlarging the understanding of the less knowledgeable. In the accounts of Matthew and Mark *proslambano* is used for Peter's taking Jesus aside. It indicates that Peter acts as if he was the one who knew what Messiahship should imply and has to put Jesus right on the matter! Note, in contrast, an appropriate use of the word: In Acts 18.26 Apollos from Alexandria taught accurately the things concerning Jesus. But he had known only the 'baptism of John'. So Priscilla and Aquila took him in hand and explained the way of God more completely. '*Proslambano*' words are used for the gracious acceptance by the Creator of the created, the less knowledgeable by the more knowledgeable, the weaker by the stronger. Peter is depicted by Mark as the one who acts as if he knows what is appropriate for a Messiah.

Now, if we had a close friend who foretold a horrible death for himself or herself, we might well seek to propose a kinder fate. But Jesus takes the intervention more seriously, and repudiates Peter's suggestion roughly, rebuking him, in turn. 'Get out of my sight, Satan' is his response to the one who had earlier confessed his

Messiahship! This he does so that the other disciples who are within hearing would take note so that Peter's rejection of the way of the cross might not infect them; and he goes on to say that that way is one which all his followers must be prepared to take.

I see an aspect of Peter's character becoming more dominant from this point. Peter becomes more assertive and at the same time more baffled about Messiahship and about his own role. There is a jostling related to power places. In chapter 10 the sons of Zebedee make a bid for places of honour in Christ's Kingdom. In contrast, Doubting Thomas, hearing of Jesus' expected death, said to fellow disciples, 'Let us also go that way that we may die with him' (John 11.16). Two aspects of power-play, self-exalting and self-sacrificing, are at work.

John alone gives the story of the foot-washing. Jesus takes the position of a household slave, kneeling before the disciples with towel and basin. It is more than Peter can stomach. The anointed one should not demean himself so. 'You shall never wash my feet' is his response. Jesus says that the washing has to do with sharing his life. Peter, seemingly not recognising that that meant accepting a lowly status, blurts out: 'Not only my feet but also my hands and my head.' Jesus points out that those who have bathed need only the dust of the road washed away – the baptised do not need re-baptism, only forgiveness and restoration. Peter is more comfortable with the idea of total cleansing (a religious requirement) than with Jesus being ranked with slaves (a social downgrading).

Peter's action at the Mount of Olives is a brave and desperate one. Mark's account simply says 'one of those standing by' drew his sword and cut off the ear of the High Priest's servant. John 18.10 identifies the attacker as Peter himself. When Peter thrice denies being a follower of Jesus, I wonder if he is still hoping that Jesus will once more turn the tables on his foes as he had so often done in the past. I think of Dietrich Bonhoeffer giving the Hitler salute in order to have space and time to assault the Nazi regime. Only afterwards does Peter, caught on one foot by the rush of events, realise the full implication of what he has done in the heat of the moment. He goes out and weeps bitterly.

In the resurrection stories, the penny does not seem to drop with Peter. He goes away from the tomb scratching his head. This was not the kind of triumphing that he had anticipated, and he seems unable, at first, to adjust. Even when Jesus makes breakfast on the shore, Peter needs to have his eyes instructed by 'the disciple whom Jesus loved' to recognise him.

After breakfast, the tone of the narrative suggests to me that something is going on other than what at first appears. Jesus gives Peter three opportunities to confess his love for him. Good: these balance the three betrayals. But why does Jesus press home 'Feed and tend my sheep and lambs'? It is as if Peter had taken his eyes off the ball. He had to be reminded of a pastoral calling. Was he getting too concerned about his own status to the detriment of pastoral duties? To me it rather sounds like a warning to Peter that he must subdue leadership ambitions to whatever is required to tend and nourish the flock. Peter's tendency to lose focus is immediately shown when he asks, pointing to the beloved disciple: 'What about him?' Jesus replies effectively: 'None of your business. Keep concentrated – you are to follow me; that is your business: feed the flock.'

That Jesus should choose women to be the primary witnesses to his resurrection was not on the messianic agenda of the disciples. They treated their testimonies as 'idle tales'. But then Jesus confirmed what they had said by his appearances. It must have been galling, in light of the low status given to women.

He goes on to instruct the disciples in the things of his Kingdom, and tells them to wait in Jerusalem for the promise of the Father. Peter was not good at waiting. Perplexed by events, he said, 'I'm going fishing.' The others joined in. The resumption of earlier, creative activity must have given settlement to minds and bodies in the tension of the resurrection events. But here, instead of waiting, Peter tries to assert his leadership, suggesting that Judas needs to be replaced.

It could be that 12 disciples provided a reminder of the 12 tribes of Israel and the need to be instructed in the New Way. Those of us who have had experience of group work know that the number 12 is about the maximum size for a continuing group which can become a fellowship of learning and serving – the purpose for which the disciples were chosen. But to reduce the members to 11 would not impair the group's effectiveness. Why did Peter propose that there be a 12th, instead of waiting in Jerusalem 'for the promise of the Father'?

For one thing, I think he needed to take initiatives to re-establish his position of leadership. For another, it was not in his nature to hang around, idle. But a third possibility is suggested by John Henson: He wanted to make sure that the 12th man *was* a man. It was disturbing to have women getting prominence by their testimony to the resurrection. They had been there all the time, a support team, but had kept a low profile, as was appropriate for mere women! What if Jesus' rehabilitation of women, asserting their equal dignity with men, should result in Jesus returning and calling a woman to be a member of the apostolic band! Peter could not wait. He may well have wanted to ensure that discipleship remained a male establishment. He got what he wanted. (That is only one among other explanations for his hasty action, but it remains a possible one.)

Once Pentecost comes, Peter shows his mettle. He puts right the mockers, identifying the agent of new light and life as God's Spirit, poured out upon all flesh. He faces up to authorities and is jailed. He welcomes Cornelius, and responds to a vision which opens the community of faith to Gentiles as well as Jews. He is perceptive, brave and unbowed.

At the same time he has to learn to accept change. Leadership in the church becomes more widely distributed than it was in the apostolic band. Paul notes four influences which were fundamental for churches in Corinth. Paul does not dismiss these, but simply insists that they must not be divisive of Christ's Lordship. At the Council of Jerusalem, Peter puts the case for the church becoming open to Gentiles. The one who presides and sums up is James, the Lord's brother. Paul becomes the great missionary to the Gentiles, and is prepared to rebuke Peter when he gives in to the circumcision party and stops eating with Gentiles, influencing others to do the same (Galatians 2.11–14) – one of the situations when the name 'Rocky' may be justified. Peter has to learn to accept multiple leadership in the fast-growing church.

By the time Paul appears on the scene there has been some tampering with the tradition (see 1 Corinthians 15.3–8). The women testifying to the resurrection have been airbrushed out. The tradition, as Paul received it, made Peter the first witness – Peter who went away from the tomb scratching his head, unable to make out what had happened; Peter who scorned the witness of the women as did all the disciples; Peter who needed to have his eyes instructed to identify Jesus, the figure cooking fish on the shore! But for the gospel accounts, the witness of the women might have got lost altogether!

It may be pointed out that, at that time, there were taken to be two spheres of life. Public matters belonged to the male sphere, so, it is argued, it would be quite in order to make the testimony of males the one which mattered. Women had their own domestic sphere; it was there that their work counted.

The death and resurrection of Jesus were certainly matters of public concern. But Jesus broke through the glass ceiling of separation, treating women as human beings of equal dignity with men, breaking with convention. When Jesus said 'follow me' to Peter and others, he meant it to apply to total discipleship, not one with a get-out clause allowing the devaluation of women to continue in the New Society. Male assertiveness had got to work on the tradition! Jesus had restored God's original intention as set out in the first chapters of Genesis. It was in their togetherness that God put women and men in charge of the earth to manage it as stewards and trustees. Paul reaffirms this, declaring that women and men are one in Christ Jesus (Galatians 3.28).

(I suppose it may be impossible to sort out now what was Paul's original text and what might have been inserted by a copyist: The demand that women be silent in church contradicts what Paul says elsewhere about all being one body in Christ, male and female. In the New Revised Standard Version, Corinthians 14.33b–36 is put in brackets. It looks like an insertion – vv 33a and 37 are in continuity.)

Jesus was never even supposed to speak to a Samaritan woman. His conversation with her made her a missionary. To a woman taken in adultery, Jesus did not offer condemnation but freed her from stoning, asking her to sin no more. He tested the mettle of the Syro-Phoenician woman who pled for her daughter, and then responded with healing, quite possibly getting a signal in the process that the time had come to be no longer constrained by a mandate focussed on the lost sheep of the House of Israel – but to be prepared to be lifted up in order that all humanity be drawn to him (1 Corinthians 15.3–8).

I come to the conclusion that Peter is divided. There is a full acknowledgment of Jesus Christ's Lordship, bravely proclaimed in word and deed; yet difficulty in accepting the terms of a way of life which would reduce his prominence, and even bring women forward into full partnership with men.

I wonder if Peter, judging Jesus (against all popular labels placed on him) to deserve the title of Messiah, became overconfident about his own perceptiveness and place. I wonder, in particular, if he resented the bringing forward of women in the life of the church.

Fresh insight on these matters now comes to me from a re-reading of 'The Lost Gospels'.

The Gospels of Mary (Magdalene), Thomas and Philip and the 'Wisdom of Faith' and 'Dialogue of the Saviour' consistently treat Mary as a specially trusted disciple.

Only in recent history have enough fragments of these ancient texts been found and skilfully reconstructed to enable us to recover what had been lost, either deliberately or unintentionally. In 1896 a fragmentary copy of the Gospel of Mary was discovered. In 1945, in Egypt, an Arab digging out soil which had fertilising properties, unearthed a huge jar which contained fragments of a dozen manuscripts, including those indicated above. So we now have access to material which had been lost for centuries. The language used was Coptic; translations were from original Greek versions.

My concern is with the question whether, from the earliest days of the church, there was strong central control of the tradition which was handed down throughout generations, which allowed male dominance to appear to be required for the church's leadership.

There are matters which I do not pursue:

a)  Dan Brown's conjecture in *The Da Vinci Code* that Jesus married Mary Magdalene and that they had children. That is to fabricate evidence, letting several angels of speculation dance on the point of a non-existent pin of reality.

b)  The contention of Gnostics in the third century that Mary was the symbolic bride of Christ. In the book of Revelation the church is the bride.

c)  The question whether, in the painting of the Last Supper, the person beside Jesus might be a woman, with Mary believed to be the likeliest candidate.

I am simply concerned to examine the judgement of the theologian Dr Tina Halkes on the way women in the New Testament are treated: 'They have stolen our names' (i.e. presence, identity, the part played). Is that so unlikely when we know that the testimony of women to the resurrection of Jesus was dismissed by the male disciples as 'idle tales'?

What is fresh in these records which had been lost out of sight for centuries?

'The Lost Gospels' testify that between the Resurrection and the Ascension Mary plays a leading part which Peter sees as a threat to his own leadership. It is not that she goes out of her own way to threaten. She merely does what is given her to do. But Peter resents the way in which other disciples treat her as a source of wisdom. He simply classifies her as 'mere woman': As a mere woman she should not be given the place which is rightly his.

Mary is depicted as more intimate with the risen Christ than others; and thus able to read his mind with a depth of understanding which others cannot match. She takes the disciples in hand when they still fear the authorities, rallies them, encourages them to face dangers and go out and proclaim the gospel. They listen and respond by 'turning their hearts to the good'. The Gospel of Mary goes on to show Peter asserting: 'The Lord loved you more than other women.' Jesus and she got their heads together in an intimate way. Peter asks her: 'Tell us what he shared with you.' Mary does so, and stirs Peter's ire! He flings out: 'Did he really speak privately with a woman and not openly to us? Are we supposed to turn round and all listen to her? Did he love her more than us?' Mary is upset that Peter reacts with rage: 'My brother Peter, what do you think? Do you think I thought this up myself in my heart or that I am lying about the Saviour?' Levi breaks in at that point, observing, 'Peter, you have always been hot-tempered. Now I see you in contention with the woman as with an enemy. But if the Saviour made her worthy, who are you to reject her? Surely the Lord knew her very well – that is why he loved her more than us.'

A similar rift is shown in 'saying 114' of the Gospel of Thomas. Jesus is present. Peter says to him: 'Tell Mary to leave us, for women are not worthy of life!' Jesus rebukes him and declares: 'I will make Mary a living spirit.'

The dialogue 'Wisdom of Faith' depicts Mary asking many questions of Jesus. Peter interrupts, irritated that Mary is hogging the conversation when he and the other male disciples should have a prior claim. Jesus rebukes him once more. Mary shares her unhappiness with Jesus at Peter's reactions: 'Peter makes me hesitant. I am afraid of him as he hates females as such.'

What irks Peter is that Mary does not fit into his category of 'mere woman'. In 'Dialogue of the Saviour' Jesus meets with three disciples, Matthew, Thomas and Mary. Mary's part in the conversation is rated highly: 'This she said as the woman who understood all things.' Peter resents the fact which others value – that a mere woman gets deeper than others in appreciation of God's mind and purpose. Yet this judgement picks up from the Old Testament where Wisdom is feminine, *Sophia*, and is related to God thus: 'I was daily his delight, rejoicing before him always, rejoicing in his inhabited world and delighting in the human race' (Proverbs 8.30, 31). To the Hebrew way of thinking Wisdom was not a 'Know-all' but a 'Perceive-deeply' character and feminine.

It irked Peter that Mary had such a warm relationship with Jesus in that post-resurrection period. In the Gospel of Philip she is described as the *suzugos*, 'yoke-fellow', of Jesus (the word can be used of a spouse but is more often used for any close committed relationship, such as between David and Jonathan). There are blanks in the following recovered passage in Philip's Gospel but the main thrust is clear: 'The *suzugos* of the Saviour is Mary Magdalene … her more than … the disciples, and used to kiss her on her [a word is lost] … The rest of the disciples were offended by this. They said "Why do you love her more than all of us?" The Saviour answered and said to them: "Why, do I not love you as much as I love her?"'

Jesus developed a specially intimate relationship with Mary after the resurrection – is this so strange? Mary had stood by the cross with Salome and the other Mary (the mother of James and Joseph) in a small group of those who had 'followed Jesus and provided for him'. They saw his body placed in a cave-tomb. Mary had been chosen by Jesus for his first appearance after the resurrection. Jesus unlocked potential in those whose lives had been changed by his love. It would be like Jesus to give a crucial role to someone who had been disregarded and discarded as beyond the pale.

It is also worth noting that when Jesus appears to Mary she does not greet him as a lover, but as a teacher: *'Rabboni'*. Also that Jesus asks her not to cling to him, because he had not yet ascended – the 'not yet' indicating that the Ascension would not mean removal of his presence but a closer intimacy than before.

To me observations in these manuscripts not only sound authentic but make sense of parts of scripture where I felt that further clarification was needed.

## Eve, the bogey woman

The brilliant stories with which Genesis starts vividly describe the relationships of God to creation, especially the human part; of human beings to one another; and of human beings to the animal kingdom and the natural order. The hymnic form of chapter 1 ('look at this, that and the other aspects of creation; isn't it marvellous?; God was pleased') served to direct praise to God; and to reveal that women and men had been chosen as God's agents and yoke-fellows to take the creation in charge, as those made in God's image in their togetherness.

In the following two chapters of Genesis, the different complementary roles of men and women are looked at. This is a point at which a lack of biblical serious-ness meets up in history with a desire for male domination. What keeps being pinpointed is that Eve took and shared the forbidden fruit. This is fastened on to make out that women are secondary players in the game of life, and unreliable ones at that. But if the whole text is attended to, it will be seen that, while Every-man/Adam and Life Source/Eve make up one humanity, it is Eve who is depicted as the stronger partner.

Play can be made of the fact that Adam came first (1 Timothy 2.13) – as if that gave him a claim to superiority. But in chapter one of Genesis we start with 'the earth was a formless void and darkness covered the face of the deep'. God said: 'Let there be light', and there was light. Does the fact that a formless void came first in time mean that it is superior to God-given light?

It is more likely that our poet theologian, Robert Burns, got it right when he spoke of the creative force of nature, thus:

> Her 'prentice han' she try'd on man,
> An' then she made the lasses, O …

The picture drawn is of Adam being made of mixed stuff, dust of the earth and God's in-breathing. Eve is depicted as being shaped from Adam's rib – a suggestion of their side-by-sideness which also asserts that she is formed of totally human stuff, in contrast with man's mixed origins. Adam, finding no yoke-fellow among animals, wakens to the reality of Eve and shouts: 'Bingo! We're of the same human stock. She is *ishshah* to my *ish* – we complete one another!' There are translators who take this as a sign of male authority established over the female. But Adam does not name Eve as he names animals. The verb used is not active but passive. He says: 'This is what I find her to be.' They discover togetherness, in accord with the mandate at the end of chapter 1.

In so many cultures the woman has to go where the man is; to be married and fit in there, sometimes being subject to the mother-in-law. The opposite is described in the biblical story. The man leaves father and mother to become one flesh (one humanity).

In the third chapter, the Tempter is shown picking on the woman as if she will be the harder nut to crack. So it proves. She meets his first attempt to undermine her by correcting the understanding of God which he proposes. The Tempter asks, 'You are not to eat from any tree in the garden?' She replies, 'We are free to eat the fruit – with one exception. If we eat the fruit of the tree which God has forbidden, it is death for us.' Only then does the Tempter strike home: 'God knows you'll not die – you will know good and evil as God does.' She gives in, and shares the fruit with Adam. The writer of the letter to Timothy comments: 'Adam was not deceived but the woman was deceived and became a transgressor.' Adam not deceived? He knew the command. He did not even question the eating of the fruit

– Eve at least put up some resistance. To blame women for all ills of life on this basis has been a sign that any old reading of the Bible will do if you need it to bolster a machismo position.

What is addressed in the parable includes the persistent human refusal to accept the intention of God – the togetherness, calling for equal partnership of men and women at all levels from the intimate to the sharing of major political, social, industrial and ecclesiastical responsibilities. The refusal is not only reprehensible. It is sinful. The church has shared in such sin from earliest times.

In Celtic mythology there is a reinstatement of the quality of life and firmness of purpose of women which reminds me of Eve. In her book *The Battle of the Birds and Other Celtic Tales*, Marion Lochhead begins her Preface thus:

> *'In Celtic legend there are always the two countries: the actual Scotland, Ireland, Wales, or Brittany – and the land of enchantments lying close to it. To pass from one to the other is easy, dangerously easy. It may happen to a quite ordinary and humble character, or to a prince. They all live on the borders of magic, king and fisherman, prince, farmer, and miller.*
>
> *Many of these stories are distinctly feminist. The hero plays his part very well – up to a point. Then he is set an impossible task, and the heroine has to come to his aid. She has courage, resourcefulness, and patience. Sometimes, within sight of a happy ending, the hero is bewitched and forgets; again the faithful girl must rescue him – as she does in The Battle of the Birds and in The Brown Bear of Norway – and forgive his lapse. It is rare for the heroine to slip; when she does, she makes full expiation. The princess in The Brown Bear of Norway is indeed misguided when she follows the advice of her mother and sisters (advice given, though they do not suspect this, by the witch) but she atones through her long journey, through patience and wisdom.'*[20]

In my own Church of Scotland, which is catholic and Reformed, we barred women from ordination till recently. The Church of Scotland now has *'an order of presbyters, male and female, ministers of the Word and Sacrament (also known as priests in large sectors of the universal church) and also an order of deacons, male and female, servants of the Lord and of his whole church'.*[21] The quality of the service of women in these capacities has led the church to kick itself that it did not see the light sooner!

## Hindrances

## c) Protectiveness of present power positions

In his day Cardinal Basil Hume contacted me with a request. Would Jan Kerkofs of *Pro Mundi Vita* magazine and I be willing to meet with himself and some monseigneurs, and spend some hours simply informing them about basic ecclesial communities springing up in different parts of the world? (I was working with the World Council of Churches at the time.) We were glad to do so.

At first the eyes of the company assembled lit up. They were hearing of a church against which the Gates of Hell would not prevail, always growing from deep roots – so that, if a winter of faithlessness blackened out the landscape, spring would follow and new green shoots cover the land.

There came a change when the question was raised about relationships with church authorities. There were cases, in Cuernavaca, Mexico, and in Ipil, in Mindanoa in the Philippines, for instance, where whole dioceses were patterned on the basis of these small Christian communities; but we had to be honest about the cases where their development was looked on as a threat, where relationships were cold and uncomprehending – hostility coming, when it did come, from traditional authorities. It was as if there developed a dawning realisation that this new growth of church might be awkward and uncomfortable to live with, in all its freshness and dynamic faith. In the end Cardinal Hume asked one of the monseigneurs to be responsible for follow-up. That was the last which was heard of it.

The church goes forward and backward, adventuring and playing safe, authorities sometimes co-operative, sometimes cagey about sprouts of new life in the grassroots. I believe it is time to take with fresh seriousness the challenge of COPE-CIAL and the World Council of Churches in the 1960s, recognising that their work on lay ministry is biblically grounded.

## Hindrances

### d) Power bids: Vatican II and a papal cuckoo

I mourn the erosion of the spirit of the Vatican II Council. It was a gift and stimulus to Christians in *every* tradition.

Pope John XXIII meant it to be an *aggiornamento*: 'bringing the church up-to-date'. He longed for church unity. Observers, invited to be part of the proceedings from other denominations, could contribute informally as real participants. It was at least a move towards the restoration of full Ecumenical Councils.

It was a time to rejoice in a Council which brought committed and imaginative minds to bear on the mandate and mission of the church in the modern world. But then these liberated and liberating minds were cut off when the Council ended. The work went into the 'play safe' and 'batten-down-the-hatches' hands of the Curia. The riots and near revolutions of 1968 scared Cardinal Ratzinger and others. Italian participants who had voted against most progressive measures in the Council saw their chance. The cry went up that the loosening-up work of the Council was producing chaos. Restoration of features of the old order was demanded. From the liberating experience of Vatican II we began to enter on *'an age which advances progressively backwards'* (T.S. Eliot, 'The Rock').

Cardinal Ratzinger laid a larger than usual egg in the ecclesiastical nest in his *Dominus Jesus*, in 2000. As Pope Benedict XVI, he then prescribed a cuckoo-like elimination of other nestlings: They do not have an equal claim to be valid occupants of the church nest. This claim, along with the reinstatement of the Latin Mass (for whatever reason?), tells against the openness of Vatican II.

Benedict XVI twists to his purpose the very word for church, *ecclesia*. It indicates the gathering of people of one mind, without barriers to admission. He allies himself with sects which claim to be the one true church. He does not do justice to church history.

A curious admirer of a commanding preacher of a bygone age once got access to the text of one of his sermons. At one point, in the margin, he found a scribble: 'Argument weak here. Shout like blazes.' This is the approach which Pope Benedict adopted. It is designed to put other churches on the defensive, and distract from weaknesses in the position of his church. These weaknesses go back to the very beginnings, and are patent today.

The mandate given by Jesus to 'the apostles whom he had chosen' was 'go into the world and proclaim the good news to the whole creation'. The result was, in one tradition, declared to be the emergence of churches threaded together by a continuous priestly succession, which authenticated them and on which they depended. St Peter thought differently. His perception was confirmed by Vatican II, which held that the definitive priesthood in concert with the High Priesthood of Jesus Christ is that of the whole people of God. To this, other priesthoods are auxiliary. Their work is to challenge, nourish and give support at the heart of the priestly people, not undermine their common priestly calling.

To elevate another priesthood and use that as a guarantee of the authenticity of a church is to usurp the place of Jesus Christ. He alone has the right to judge who are genuinely his people.

A final point about Pope Benedict's power-push: Even Orthodox churches are said to suffer from a '*defectus*' because they do not accord primacy to the Pope. Why should they? In the early churches there were four centres of orthodox faith: Jerusalem (accorded primacy by Celtic monastic communities), Antioch, Alexandria, and Rome; later joined by Constantinople (Istanbul). Different histories, cultures, forms of human experience were thus able to contribute to a rich orthodoxy. To make one centre dominant would be to impose a straitjacket into which life would need to be squeezed. In Galatians 5, Paul warns: 'For freedom Christ has set us free – don't submit to old forms of bondage.' Jesus warned against the top-down power exercised by rulers of the Gentiles, who wanted to have their way and still be treated as benefactors. Servant power is different.

The only positive thing which comes out of this contemporary push for power is this: It represents another nail in the coffin of papal infallibility. This juvenile 'king of the castle' theology is not worth the attention of serious minds. It is a push-and-shove game you might find in children's playgrounds.

Of all people, Pope Benedict XVI should be prepared to listen to fresh challenges – such as those offered by Brazilian bishop Pedro Casaldaliga, who, in a Fraternal Circular Letter sent as we entered this millennium, wrote: '*The reform of the papacy and the Curia would make possible – with the 'autonomy' of the Spirit and the expectations of the universal Church – many reforms in co-responsibility, collegiality, inculturation, legitimate pluralism, and in ministries.*'[22] The present Pope was the one who, as Cardinal Ratzinger, observed in his book *The New People of God*: '*The church needs men with passion for the truth and prophetic denunciation. Christians ought to be critical even in regard to the Pope himself, because certain panegyrics do* great harm to the Church and to him.'[23]

So am I anti-Catholic? The opposite. For me, brought up in a catholic and Reformed tradition, the church which is catholic in the Roman tradition was a positive, great discovery.

Whenever I have encountered Roman Catholics in the ninety-five countries in which I have had some assignment, I have been welcomed as one of themselves. I delight in that church, rejoice in its faithful witness, and do not want to see it move backwards. I take my place among those of that communion who seek an alternative to the top-down, laity-disinheriting model. I am simply going alongside many, many thoughtful Roman Catholics who want the *aggiornamento* to continue, not to be suppressed.

In a recent article, 'Thy Kingdom Come', published in *The Social Edge*, Ted Schmidt, former editor of the *New Catholic Times*, gives a view of the post-Vatican II Church. He observes: '*The extraordinary efflorescence of the Church with its new birth in the halcyon days of the 1960s has been stalemated at its highest institutional levels … It was naive to believe that a Church which redefined itself as the "People of God", with all its inclusiveness of baptism, would not be resisted by a clerical culture – secretive, exclusive, patriarchal and hierarchical.*'

Schmidt also mourns the stepping back from '*the protection of the* anawim, *the voiceless ones, those with no power*'. He lauds the role of Pope Paul VI, and quotes from his *Evangelium Nuntiandi* (1975): '*Only the kingdom is absolute … and it makes everything else relative.*' (That covers the papacy, sacraments, the Bible, priesthood, the church: Only God's reign of peace and justice is ultimate.)

In contrast, when Pope John Paul II followed on '*… the "Pope's men", cautious, conservative, chancery types, were imposed on dioceses …*' Schmidt quotes Notre Dame theologian Richard McBrien, who wrote in the *New York Times*: '*These bishops tend to be uncritically loyal to the Pope and his curial associates, rigidly authoritarian and solitary in the exercise of pastoral leadership …*'

Ted Schmidt adds: '*Baptism inaugurates a kingdom of equals – yet patriarchy, hierarchy and clericalism continue to deform the Body … The issues that exercise kingdom Catholics are seldom dogmatic and mainly involve church governance (parish control, lay leadership) and discipline (celibacy, female ordination) all of which could be changed, as Pope John XXIII said, by a stroke of a pen.*'[24]

'We Are Church', 'Catholics for a Changing Church' and 'Déclaration du Peuple

Qui Fait Eglise' advocate measures which would establish a more authentic orthodoxy.

## Into the hands of the people

God is not neutral. Jesus' mother, Mary, saw this clearly:

> 'He has brought down the powerful from their thrones
> and lifted up the lowly;
> he has filled the hungry with good things
> and sent the rich away empty.'

The realisation that God seeks liberation from oppression for the whole human race finds new expression in our time. One of the gifts of the Vatican II Council was to put the scriptures into the hands of the people, instead of keeping them in 'safe' priestly hands. Biblical references are clear and direct in the *Misa Tipica*, the indigenous mass which draws upon the experience of basic people in Central America. Their own images contrast the will of God with the reality they have to live – and as Western, abstract language cannot. I stayed in the Ciudad Sandino in Nicaragua and took part in the celebrations which marked the first anniversary of the success of the revolution. Worship was a stimulus to drastic change.

In the Creed of the Mass of Nicaraguan Farmers, we find:

> 'I believe in you,
> my companion,
> the human Christ, the worker Christ,
> the conqueror of death.
> By your measureless sacrifice
> you have begotten the new human being
> who is destined for liberation.
> You are living
> in every arm raised
> to defend the people
> against exploitative domination;
> because you are alive on the ranch,
> in the factory, in the school.
> I believe in your truceless struggle,
> I believe in your resurrection.'

The Kyrie, the 'Lord, have mercy' cry, is

*'Christ, Christ Jesus,*
*be one with us.*

*Lord, Lord my God,*
*be one with us.*

*Christ, Christ Jesus,*
*take sides*
*not with the oppressor class*
*that squeezes dry and devours*
*the community,*
*but with the oppressed,*
*with my people*
*thirsting for peace.'*

## Hindrances

### e) Ecumenical assignments relegated to the background
*A reflection on Scottish Churches House, the house of the churches together in Dunblane*

When representatives of different churches appraised the result for Scotland of the formation of the World Council of Churches, they came to the conclusion that what was needed in their own land was a house of the churches together to be a sign and instrument of unity. The sign would be that, besides the formation of the Ecumenical Committee (official appointees) and the Ecumenical Association (grassroots enthusiasts) which worked closely together, there would be a common base, a springboard for ecumenical advance. The instrument would provide means to serve the world with integrity, get down to work on the kind of unity to be sought and on differences which were proving to be barriers, and make discoveries in the life of prayer and devotion.

That was fifty years ago. It is a time for fresh appraisal.

The House has proved its capacity to serve the world with integrity using lay resources with fresh imagination and flair. It can bring together people well instructed in the faith, equipped with the different experiences and competences required, to join with equivalents in society who do not hold Christian positions, to address large matters of common concern and move life forward. It has made explorations in the life of prayer and devotion. But the churches have little used it as a common instrument to deal with the unity sought and differences which block the way.

Suppose the ecumenical calling were taken with full seriousness, what would it mean?

The ecumenical movement would not be treated like a trailer attached to churches which allowed them to continue with separate development while in tolerant association with one another – a trailer which can be unhitched when the financial going gets tough.

The ecumenical assignment is made quite explicit in Jesus Christ's prayer, 'As you, Father, are in me and I am in you, may they be one in us, so that the world may believe that you sent me' (John 17.21). That is deep-driving stuff!

a) 'As you, Father, are in me and I am in you, may they be one in us …': Churches must reject the temptation to find security and fulfilment in the form or forms which they have taken in history and be prepared to die as they have been to enter into a unity which expresses more adequately that of the Father and Son. 'Reconciled Diversity' may provide a stepping stone across the stream of tradition to a land of greater commitment – but you don't rest on stepping stones. This prayer is apt:

> *Lord God*
> *whose son was content to die*
> *to bring new life,*
> *have mercy on your church*
> *which will do anything you ask,*
> *anything at all,*
> *except die and be reborn.*
>
> *Lord Christ,*
> *forbid us unity*
> *which leaves us where we are*
> *and as we are:*
> *welded into one company*
> *but extracted from the battle;*
> *engaged to be yours*
> *but not found at your side.*

*Holy Spirit of God,*
*reach deeper than our inertia and fears,*
*release us into the freedom*
*of children of God.*

b) ' … that the world may believe that you have sent me.':

- The world is given no incentive to believe that Jesus is the emissary of the Father wherever it sees full participation in the sacrament of unity – which he left to nourish and bind and build up the church – debarred in principle from fellow Christians.

- The world will not believe if in this or that church it sees males monopolise decision-making. (In the Old Testament, the very first chapter of the Bible portrays God conferring the management of creation, as trustees and stewards, on women and men together. In the New Testament Paul avers that no distinction in status is to be made between male and female – we are 'all one in Christ Jesus'.) There is a glaring gulf between belief and practice.

- The world will not believe that Jesus was reflecting the mind of the Father when he took and advocates servant status, when they see his people represented by different kinds of eminences, deferred to and given clout in church and in public. The church is grassroots movement as well as institution.

  Or where laity are made a category, often a subservient one.

  Or where authority alongside the supreme authority of Jesus Christ is vested in the whole Spirit-gifted people of God, yet is so often exercised over their heads!

- The world has no incentive to believe that we are one in Christ Jesus wherever, apart from a few hopeful experiments, equipping for the life of faith is separately undertaken in schools, seminaries and theological colleges.

  Or where leadership of 'apostles, prophets, evangelists, pastors and teachers', provided 'to equip the saints' (i.e. the ordinary Christian punters) for the work of ministry, is not given priority.

- The world will fail to believe if it sees official institutions treating grassroots Christian movements as having no legitimacy, when the church began bottom-up in its earliest years, in house churches, not top-down.

Matters such as these should no longer be left to professional and ordained ecclesiastical representatives. So many of us come into dialogue heavily weighed down with assumptions sacred to different traditions that we soon get gummed up. These are matters for Christians of all kinds to take up in a fresh drive for fuller unity.

When there was an institutional move to sell off Scottish Churches House, I was open to conviction that the House might have had its day. You don't carry on projects which played their part in the past just because they continue to exist. But there was the Appeal, and four hundred people put their money where their mouth was to say the House of Churches Together was at least as urgently needed today as it had been in the past.

Major ecumenical challenges have to be faced and dealt with if the world is to be convinced that Jesus Christ came into it as God's emissary and called us into unity with the Father and with one another. Means for doing so in Scotland are at hand. It is time to re-appropriate them.

But we are in a new period of history. The challenges which face a new generation will mean picking up, in a fresh way, significant concerns of the past and also forming a fresh agenda for the future.

*Church in the becoming*

# RECONCILED DIVERSITY

When I was a student, the main goal of the ecumenical movement was organic church union. But it was difficult to picture what that would mean and to discern how to achieve it. Could there be one pattern of church life which in every part of the world would gather into it the essential features which marked the church of Jesus Christ? Would such an accepted pattern rob the churches of characteristics which, at certain points of their development, helped them to get a clearer picture of what the gospel required of them? Would one of the historic forms of church be liable to dominate – when I interviewed Ian Paisley in the grounds of the House of Commons many moons ago he flatly declared that the ecumenical movement was a slide towards Rome! What is more, in discerning essential marks of the church, how are we to distinguish idiosyncrasy from heresy?

This latter question is addressed by Clodovis Boff in *The Catholic Church and the New Churches in Latin America* (2008). He starts with this declaration: *'Our ultimate horizon will always be ecumenism: how can we come together in the Church and how can we come together in the social mission of the churches?'*[25] He clearly sees that ecumenism is not just about churches seeking unity between themselves. To cosy up to one another could be a betrayal of the gospel, a search for security over against self-giving for the world God loves.

He examines the rise of Pentecostalism in Latin America and the decline of his own church. (I myself learned to appreciate the qualities of Pentecostalism when I used as a base for work in Central America the Pentecostal centre in Barquisimeto, Venezuela.)

Clodovis acknowledges in full how the witness of Pentecostals shows up the inadequacies in the life and witness of his church, its failure to relate imaginatively and sensitively to many of the needs of the people, especially the poor. He then looks at the largest and fastest-growing Pentecostal church, the 'Universal Church of the Kingdom of God'. He notes that it *'is built on three pillars, healing, exorcism and the theology of prosperity, which conveys the following message: "God wants us to be rich, lucky, healthy, successful".'*[26] How about Jesus' word: 'You cannot serve God and Mammon'? Do not most churches hold to stances and emphases which are questioned by others? How could they come into one communion?

Churches with different denominational traditions may grow together over the years. Churches in the West End of Edinburgh have shown mutual respect for one another and gained maturing understanding over many decades. They have now entered into a covenant relationship with explicit common commitments: outreach to society's financial and retail sectors, engagement with the arts, and interfaith work. They do not merge, giving up their particular traditions, but simply develop the ministry of the people of God in explicit partnership with one another.

By the time of the Faith and Order Conference in Louvain in 1971, the concept of the ecumenical goal as being 'reconciled diversity' was more to the fore. 'Churches Together' seems to me to be a current way of expressing this. The Edinburgh West End churches simply call themselves 'Together'.

'Reconciled diversity', once accepted, can encourage churches to learn from one another's traditions, without devaluing their own, and to grow outwards.

I think in particular of the example provided by Canonmills Church in Edinburgh. It is unusual in that it has no ordained pastor-in-charge. Its co-ordinator of ministries was, at one time, the late Tom Fleming (actor, producer, radio and TV commentator). Some of us who are ordained serve from time to time. On one such occasion, when I was invited to be available throughout Holy Week, I asked, at the end, how many of the congregation would have made particular contributions to the worship and service of the week. Tom estimated about forty. The church is a living body.

At Canonmills, I was asked to share in the baptism of a Hindu lass whose journey in life had led her to embrace the Christian faith. Canonmills is rooted in the Baptist tradition, though it calls itself by a more ecumenical designation (much as my wife, Margaret, did, who identified herself as 'a post-denominational Christian'). The immersing of the lass in the baptismal pool, and her rising to join the local congregation, said more clearly than a font ever could that baptism signified dying to an old life and rising to a new one, a life to be lived in new community.

Two things were precious. One was the movement in the baptism. The other was a layman presiding.

While Ignatius of Antioch, early in the second century, urged that the bishop (i.e. the local pastor) preside at communion, he also said that if this were not always possible, he should nominate someone he trusted. The qualification for presiding is a profound understanding of the meaning of the sacrament and ability to convey that meaning in word and action. A layman can be so gifted – and more so than some of those of us who are ordained.

That we have, in the church catholic, a form of baptism which maturely conveys its theological meaning so clearly as that in the Baptist tradition, and a ministry which is multiple, provides a sign which remains potent for an understanding of church.

I have heard the Salvation Army dismissed as a sect by some in mainline churches. How impoverished the testimony to Jesus Christ, servant of the poor, would be without its life and witness! An update on it was provided in *The Guardian* of 17th December, 2008:

*The Salvation Army is a Christian church and charity operating in 117 countries, with 1.6 million members and 107,000 employees. It is, quite amazingly, the second largest provider of social care in Britain – after the state – care which includes giving 3,200 homeless people food and shelter every night in 57 hostels, visiting prisoners, running 17 residential centres for elderly people, 70 day centres, 50 nurseries and playgroups, a family tracing service that reunites 10 people a day with their relatives, youth clubs, employment training centres, and a centre for women escaping domestic violence. It will distribute 150,000 presents this Christmas for those, and perhaps you're one of them, who have little or nothing under their Christmas tree – if they're fortunate enough to have a tree ...*[27]

It was the Congregational Church which, in Scotland, led the way to righting a deficiency in the ordained ministry with the ordination of Vera Kenmure in 1928 – providing a sign for other churches to follow.

Where would we be without the witness of the Friends: that we need, in quiet, to wait upon God – and without their social conscience? And of the Episcopal Church of Scotland in its worship?

The time fails me ... All churches are enriching themselves by appreciating forms of worship which they come across as they gather in praise together and serve the world God loves together. Moving thus into the future they are discovering afresh that the decisive ministry in and to the world is that of the whole church, with the many resources of the Spirit in gifted people brought into play.

I think of Xavier Gorostiaga, Jesuit priest in Nicaragua who, when the culmination of the revolution against the dictatorship drew near, was told: 'There is nothing which you can do as a priest which we cannot do as a priestly people. What we need is to be better equipped in economic and financial affairs of state to build a new country. Go to Ruskin College and get sharpened up on these things – then you can be of real use to us.'

When the communists succeeded in cutting the link between Roman Catholics in Czechoslovakia and the Vatican, members were told by Rome, 'Do what you find possible' (as had earlier been done with Mexico). I was impressed with the integration of bishops and people which resulted, and remarked on the complete lack of deference, which was replaced by mutual respect and good comradeship (bishops had been jailed with the other members of the church). In reply it was said: 'But bishops Jan and Fridolin just have a job. In the church we all have jobs.'

It scares some who are in high ecclesiastical positions that the priestly people are equipped by the Spirit with all that is needed to exercise ministry.

There is one Head of the body, in which different functions are knit together by ligaments which relate them for dynamic life in the world. 'God has so arranged the body, giving the greater honour to the inferior member, that there may be no dissention within the body but the members may have the same care for one another' (1 Corinthians 12.24,25). The body is a sign of reconciled diversity.

# LIPPEN ON THE HOLY SPIRIT

The stories I tell here have already been shared as particular items at particular times. But they belong to one journey. Here I thread them into one necklace, each one in order of time. I do so because I have thought: *Should I be given the chance before I die to leave one word of advice, what would it be?* Without hesitation I knew. It would be 'Lippen on the Holy Spirit: lean on, trust in, keep turning to, develop a living relationship with the Holy Spirit'.

Faced with contemporary decisions and choices, some say, 'I must ask myself what Jesus Christ would have done in this situation.' For one thing, they don't seem to realise what a huge task they set themselves. They would need to divest these situations of contemporary factors, re-clothe them in a Palestinian first-century context and follow through with what would be prescribed as Christ-like in the present day – in my judgement an impossible task.

For another, Christ Jesus has different advice: 'When the Spirit of truth comes, he will guide you into all the truth; for he will not speak on his own authority, but will speak only what he hears and he will make known to you what is to come. He will glorify me, for he will take what is mine and make it known to you. All that the Father has is mine – and that is why I said: "He will take what is mine and make it known to you".' (John 16.13–15).

'Lippen on the Holy Spirit' is the advice of Jesus Christ Himself; for when we are faced with decisions and choices in our own time, and seek to deal with these according his mind, the Spirit will make his mind known.

How this works out is clearly illustrated in Acts 13 and 16.

At the start of Chapter 13 we are given a picture of prophets and teachers in Antioch who strenuously seek the will of the Spirit in prayer and fasting. The Holy Spirit responds with 'Set Barnabas and Paul apart for me, to do the work to which I have called them.' The work is not specified. They will find, as they take the road, what is required of them at each stage.

Features of a journey are revealed in Acts 16. Paul and his companions are prevented from delivering the message of the Church Council to inhabitants of Asia (at that time a province not a continent). What stops them? The Holy Spirit! They go on and attempt to enter Bythnia, but the way is barred again by the Holy Spirit. Paul, an evangelist to his fingertips, is denied opportunity to preach to people who did not even know the name of Jesus – by the Holy Spirit! They either skirt or go straight through Mysia, and come to Troas. There a Macedonian appears in a night vision, appealing to them to 'cross over to Macedonia and help us'. Then they 'set about getting a passage to Macedonia, convinced that God has called us to take the good news there'.

Paul and his companions were able to begin the mission to Europe only because they disciplined themselves to be attentive to the Holy Spirit both when they were told 'Speak up' and 'Shut up'. (O, that some contemporary evangelists heard the second command as well as the first! The gift they might give at times would be to step aside and to sit at the feet of ordinary people and learn what the Spirit is saying to the churches.)

The journey which I undertook in 1980 was to Mexico, Guatemala, El Salvador, Nicaragua, Panama and Venezuela, visiting basic Christian communities and carrying news of the work of the Spirit manifest in their development in different parts of the world which I had visited.

To understand what follows, it is necessary to appreciate that my and Margaret's marriage was like a coin with its two sides. On the one hand, we were given to one another to delight in one another. We had a special gift for that. We were utterly charmed, all our days, to share life. On the other hand, we were given this togetherness to fulfil Kingdom assignments. What these would be we could not anticipate. We had simply to be alert to read the signs given on the way.

Margaret was especially good at reading these signs and jaloosing what should come next. Whatever I had to do on my own (e.g. for the World Council of Churches) would get her blessing. Except in this instance! She almost dug in her heels and tried to dissuade me from this journey. The problem was that, at that time, Guatemala and El Salvador were killing fields and she knew that I would be not with protected tourists but with those counted eliminable. First she tried the line that there was enough information about these two countries available in print and I could miss them out without loss. My reply was simply that, as she knew, reports of others were not good enough – I needed to find what I needed to find. She left it a few days. Then she said that not only reports but people were coming from these two countries – I could seek them out and get direct information of the kind I wanted. I replied that, as she knew, I needed to see people and sniff out the reality of situations in their natural context, not away from it. She gave up. I went with her reluctant blessing after all.

Was it that my conviction overcame her hesitations? That was not our way. We were together-people. I believe she came to see that she was looking on our marriage as if it had only one side, the delight in one another. She was scared for my well-being, even for my life. I believe she worked things out so that she came to the point where perfect love casts out fear. She consented to what she came to see as a Kingdom assignment, part of the package which was our marriage.

The visit to Mexico was straightforward. Bishop Méndez Arceo had developed his diocese on a basis of space given for small communities to flourish. I was able to get updated about their recent history and share with them insights from the life of communities in other parts of the world.

Four hours before my flight to Guatemala my Mexican host, Dr Gaxiola Gaxiola, got a phone call. It was to say that all my contacts in Guatemala and El Salvador had been killed, or had fled the country or gone underground – there would be no one to meet me to provide links with the small communities. Dr Gaxiola suggested I had better give up on the trip and fly back to Britain. But that would have meant that an interested party would not have been consulted – the Holy Spirit. I asked leave to go away by myself for 10-15 minutes to think things through. All I did was open myself to the Spirit.

In my experience the guidance the Spirit gives is not resoundingly clear. It may edge slightly to one way rather than another way and you simply have to make a judgement and plunge. You know, in any case, that if you have chosen rightly, your initiative will be gathered into a large divine initiative, and if wrongly, that it will be covered by an entirely sufficient forgiveness. I came back to my host and said I was going to continue with the journey.

What are you to do if you land in a strange country and all your contacts (except one priest, who I knew would not be at the airport) are eliminated? If I remember rightly, the person who was originally to meet me was called Sister Angela. I approached some of those who were meeting new arrivals and asked if they had seen Sister Angela. Some did not know her, others had not seen her recently. I knew this would be so. The whole idea was to make some sort of human contact in the hope that something might come of it.

Two nuns who I approached were expecting two other nuns, who disembarked behind me. When these arrived, they all moved off in a great flurry of greetings and welcoming conversation. The word came to me 'Stand around and look forlorn'. In fact these exact words came to me. I remember the word 'forlorn' in particular. How on earth could such an irrelevant thought come from the action of the Holy Spirit? All I knew was that strange pointers like this had, in the past, proved to have substance in them which I could not see at first. At the entrance to the airport I stood around looking forlorn.

At that time the entry to parking areas and the exit from the airport were close to one another. After some time the car with the four nuns appeared, ready for departure. The driver saw forlorn me, changed direction, swung alongside and asked if Sister Angela had not turned up. When I said she had not, the nun said that there was still a spare seat in the car. They would want to help – but could only do so if the place I wanted to reach was in the direction they had to take. I mentioned Iglesia la Merced. 'No problem. That's on our way. Hop in!'

If I had taken a taxi into the centre of the city, I would have been met by a closed and darkened church and would have been quite lost. As it was, the nuns knew the church house, which was in a warren of side streets. They took me there. A priest was putting away his car. He said that if I had arrived five minutes earlier, he would not have been there. If I had arrived five minutes later, no one would have answered the door. Too often a gun had been poked through a space in the metal grill and the person who answered had been shot at. The priest was the one person whose name I still had, not only in Guatemala City but in the whole country. I was provided with a base from which to operate.

On arrival in El Salvador, I adopted a different tactic. I made for Bishop Romero's headquarters and asked around, seeking some sort of lead. I got none. I went out the front door. To the left of it was an open space about the size of a school playground. Two men were walking diagonally across it, talking. I took the chance to bring them into conversation and found that one of them was Romero's liaison link with basic Christian communities! Once again I had purchase on a situation which seemed to yield none. His companion was in charge of the Roman Catholic radio station which bravely provided knowledge of what was really happening in the country. Though it was towards shutdown time in the evening he invited me to look around before the station closed – I could leave my rucksack in one of the rooms. So we wandered across a few hundred yards and I was shown around. At shutdown I wandered back – to find that the room in which I had left my rucksack was locked for the night and no one who was still there knew how to gain entrance.

I found that this was because of a device that had been adopted. The military, hostile to Romero and all that he stood for, were liable to raid the church head-quarters without notice, looking for 'subversive material'. Evidently they were not allowed to make forced entry to particular rooms. So each room had a locking up arrangement which was not shared – so that others could genuinely tell the military that they did not know how to gain access. My rucksack was out of reach.

As the headquarters closed down, I realised I had two options. One was to sleep rough, in the open air. I was accustomed to rough sleeping. That was not the problem. The problem was death squads, wandering about at night, indiscriminately killing, leaving corpses to be picked up in the morning. The alternative was to try to get a bed in a modest residence. But I had no baggage, no airline tickets, no passport or other identification, no money – the police would be called, and Salvadorean jails were not known for their gentleness and comfort.

At that point I put my hand in my pocket – and found that Romero's basic Christian communities linkman, who lived outside the city, had given me his card, which I had pocketed without thinking. I also found some Salvadorean coins. For the life of me I cannot say how they got there – I had not bought anything which would have produced change. They were exactly the amount needed for a phone call. (George MacLeod would have said: 'If you think that is a coincidence, I wish you a very dull life!') I made contact and was told that, not far from where I was, I could find a house which a family had abandoned because of pressure from an anti-Romero military neighbour. There was still a caretaker there – he would provide a bed for the night. The next morning no one was earlier than me at the church headquarters, anxious to retrieve the signs of legitimacy and identity which the rucksack held!

In Nicaragua, I stayed first of all with Xavier Gorostiaga, the economic supremo of the new Nicaragua – produced by a brilliant people's revolution (eventually undermined and befouled by Reagan's illegal Contras and all manner of interference and dirty tricks by the USA). I had found Xavier in Ruskin College. (Developments in Nicaragua meant that he had a year to spare after Ruskin. I got him to come to Selly Oak Colleges as Third World lecturer, or something like that. We had flexibility in Selly Oak and could make appointments according to need as long as resources could be found.)

After some days in the Jesuit Centre which Xavier had as his base, I moved to Ciudad Sandino, a barrio which had four Jesuit priests at its heart, with whom I teamed up for some more days, experiencing the outburst of gratitude and hope which marked the first anniversary of the success of the revolution. From the barrio, members of basic Christian communities had gone out to join the guerrillas when they came down from the hills to capture Managua, in one instance with sticks and stones assaulting the armoured cars (48 if I remember rightly) supplied by Britain to the dictator Somoza. There could not have been, at any other point of history, such a commitment of Christian believers in a revolutionary struggle.

I then moved on to Panama. I understand how difficult it might be for some readers to credit the story which follows. All I can do is supply a record.

Sometimes I had minimal information for getting in touch with small Christian communities. They did not advertise themselves. They might be beavering away, living the faith imaginatively under the noses of the official church without that church realising that they existed.

When I had to journey (as Abraham and Paul did) on a basis 'go and I'll show you on the road what to do', I had a prayer which went something like this: *'Look, God, I may have misread signs – or maybe you want me out of the road to act through other people. If this journey appears to me to be fruitless, fair enough – you know the total scene. But if you want it to bear fruit, please put the people I need to work with in touch with me.'*

In the case of Panama, I flew in with nothing to go on except the name of the person who linked the basic Christian communities. I had no address. I might easily have spent the three days I had allowed for the visit searching without being able to find him.

This is what happened: When I was flying to Panama he was driving on some assignment well away from the airport. He experienced a very strong sensation that he was required to turn back on his tracks. He realised that such an irrational feeling must not be given weight and tried to drive on. The pressure to turn round became so strong that he yielded. He drove up to the airport just as I was coming out. We did not know one another but recognised one another at once. I found I had arrived at a rare time when the Panamanian communities had three days of interchange – not meeting in a block but visiting one another in a process of mutual learning and mutual sustaining.

Thereafter I moved on to Venezuela, to a Pentecostal centre in Barquisimeto which I used for a base and for occasional consultations. On one occasion, my awareness that something new was stirring (though words such as basic Christian communities or basic ecclesial communities were still not current) led me to set up a five-day gathering of those involved, from Puerto Rico right round to Venezuela. The provision at the centre was absolutely basic – had we met in a hotel, participants would have been tongue-tied with culture shock. In the Pentecostal centre they met at a level which did not disturb or confuse them.

While I was at Barquisimeto, I heard of shanty towns growing up around Caracas, as poor people in the countryside moved into the city to try to make a living. The concern of the Participation in Change programme, co-ordinated for the World Council of Churches, remained with me with its focus on how the poor were coping with change. So I got my ticket altered to spend a day or two in Caracas on the way back. But, try as I would, I could get no means of contact with people in Caracas, to give me entry to the shanty towns.

On the way to the plane to Caracas I took God to task, 'Look Lord, a covenant is two-sided. You have your bit to do as well as I have. So please get off your butt and do something – unless a fruitless journey is what you actually want.'

The pilot was a show-off. Never in my life have I been in a plane which took off at such a steep angle. When he straightened it out, a lass came forward from further down the plane with my plastic file in her hand. With the angle taken by the plane on take-off, it had slipped through the back of the seat beside me, and slid down to land at her feet. I thanked her. Then she said, 'I wanted an excuse to see you in any case: I think you work for the World Council of Churches in Switzerland.' I wondered furiously what committee or commission we might have worked on together. It was not that. 'It's just that, some time ago, I went on the tour of the World Council headquarters and I think I saw you there. When you came on board I recognised you. The landing of your file at my feet gave me an excuse to come and talk.'

So she sat beside me and we chatted. *Did she stay in Switzerland and have business in Caracas?* No, Caracas was her home city. She had been on a course in Switzerland which was not obtainable outside Europe, and now she was on her way back. *What type of course was it?* It was designed to equip her better for some work in the social services, her job in Caracas. *What kind of organisation did she work for? Religious, medical, political?* She was on the social services staff of Caracas City Council. *Was there any line of work for which she had particular responsibility?* Her main job was to be a liaison between the Council and the slum-dwellers in the hills around the city.

There is a mystery in all this. Did I prove to be inadequate martyr material? I was not killed even once, by death squads or by other means. I was not even jailed. I came within a whisker of that in the Philippines. The dictator Marcos had gone to spend time with his pal Ronald Reagan. Specially close watch was kept on exits for the dissemination of undesirable information! I had volunteered to carry records of assassinations, tortures, etc to London to post to different justice and peace committees in different parts of the world. They were almost found on me. That would have been rough.

Margaret never complained that I returned safely from each visit! Sure, the Holy Spirit was guide, comforter and friend. But that does not guarantee survival in this life. I shared Margaret's relief.

# Living as People of the Way

*Early on, Christians were called 'People of the Way': not because they were marshalled into a pattern of living, keeping in step in a prescribed pattern of movement – there were variations in different times and cultures – but because they had a style of life which marked them out as, in community, they faced up to life in the world.*

*At one and the same time they were called to deal unflinchingly with that world exactly as it was, and to reckon with a 'beyondness' – transcendent factors which made sense of it and gave it purpose. They were called to an openness in relating to God, to other people, to other creatures, to situations, which meant avoiding stereotypical reactions and judgements, and being teachable before unusual, unfamiliar elements in life. It is in their uniqueness and in community that people achieve at-one-ment; and through grace given.*

*As they move through life the People of the Way must show alertness to developments in the world, around their doors and further afield, which impinge on the coming of the Kingdom and the doing of God's will. Purity of life needs to be understood in biblical terms. Law and grace need to complement one another. Prayer matters. Food-sharing will be both a means of fellowship and a reminder that the resources of the world are to be shared fairly.*

*Two of the points at which choice of the path to be followed can put Christians to the test include:*

- *What Paul, in a different context, calls 'pride in outward show not in inward worth' (2 Corinthians 5.12).*

- *Sexuality treated as a pleasure-seeking element detached from its spiritual gifts for relationships, intimate and social.*

# WAIT WATCHFULLY

On one occasion, I mentioned to George MacLeod how often Jesus Christ warned those who had ears to hear to wait, alert to developments. He waved the thought away with 'That is hardly at the heart of the gospel.' Not the heart. But it is also important that the heartbeat of the gospel get full attention.

I discern behind the advice a profound theological observation. The Great Doer in earthly life is God. There is no handover to consecrated human beings. Servants of God's purposes are called to be co-workers with Jesus Christ through the Holy Spirit to enable God's will to be fulfilled. But they have to be alert to find what God is getting up to. Then they are to find at what points they are called to stay out, *and* at what points to be prepared to be shouted in, and if the latter, what particular contribution to be expected to make. Whatever light comes to an individual needs to be tested in community (as in Acts 13.1–3) – and not a community of the like-minded, but of all sorts – to check whether what is asked is really of the Holy Spirit.

The fact is that we do not know what our life is for, without the Holy Spirit revealing, stage by stage, how life is to be spent. We become truly ourselves when we are 'clothed upon' by Christ – his true nature fulfilling our given nature. Our life will be lived truly not by assessing our talents and matching them to opportunities. On that basis Paul could have evangelised in Asia, Bithynia and Mysia and missed Troas. We are not to invest life in enterprises just because they are good. Nor are we to hesitate forever at crossroads. Professor John Baillie once asked us, in class, what should be done if we came to a fork in life's road issuing in two options which, after prayer and research, seemed equally compelling. We could not answer. He suggested that we toss a coin. If at the end of all forms of consideration both ways seem equally personally challenging, we can take either; God will know the choice of either option and turn it to good. At that point I thought of a cowboy hero of my childhood in *The Rover* magazine. He came to a town where all the sheriffs who held office previously had been eliminated by bad men. The office was vacant, open to applications. He wondered if he should apply. He decided to toss a coin. If it came up heads he would put himself forward; if tails, he would not. The thirteenth time that he tossed the coin it came up heads, so he took the job.

The essence, in biblical terms, is to wait till situations are ripe – alert to be able, through the leading of the Spirit, to respond as required.

Pictures used in the Bible are of watchtowers and watchmen. In the book of Habakkuk (who takes God to task, as did Job, for mismanaging the world) there is awareness that the initiative is with God. 'I will keep watch to see what God will say to me' (2.1). The answer comes: 'There is still a vision for the appointed time. It speaks of the end and does not lie. If it seems to tarry, wait for it' (2.3). Isaiah, looking for the restoration of Jerusalem, also envisions watchmen. They are not only to take no rest, staying on the *qui vive*; they are also to pester God to take action 'until he makes Jerusalem a theme of praise throughout the world' (62.7).

To wait and watch has to go with active service. Inactive waiting is ruled out. In the New Testament the figure of a householder returning from an engagement at an unexpected hour is used to applaud servants or slaves who have remained watchful for that return, still getting on with their work. 'Blessed is that slave whom the master will find getting on with his work, when he arrives' (Luke 12.43). Another favourite picture is of the Son of Man coming like a thief in the night, so that those waiting need to have their guard up, not be found sleeping.

The Incarnation came when the time was ripe. It caught some off guard. But some were alert. Christ still comes in unexpected ways. We need to be wakeful to respond.

# TRANSCENDENCE

A sense of transcendence is necessary to give value to the human. Without it, powers-that-be can define the human to suit their interests and ambitions. What makes us human is thus degraded.

The business of dehumanising opponents has been a resort of combatants all through history – and still needs to be stamped out in chants at football matches! So we get words such as nig-nogs, wogs, yobs: if some people can be looked on as subhuman, they can, with impunity, and even with 'justice', be raped, tortured, killed!

So it is a very significant claim that every human being is created in the image of God, and should be treated accordingly.

Jesus treated people as having significance in God's sight: women at a time when they were looked on as the personal property of men, children, despised Samaritans, Gentiles who had been robbed of their place in the Temple. He said of children: 'It is to such as these that the Kingdom of God belongs.' It was the Kingdom of God that he announced – the whole fabric of created life being transformed to work God's way. In our time, protest marches against war, movements to 'Make Poverty History' and to care for planet Earth involve people quite outwith any identifiable faith as well as those who confess one. By such acts, humanity is asserted to have intrinsic God-given value not related to colour, class, creed, tribe, gender or anything else. The psalmist in Psalm 8 is full of wonder that human beings who die like beasts (Psalm 49) are given such a high ranking by God, of sheer grace:

> *What is a frail mortal that you should be mindful of him,*
> *a human being that you should take notice of him?*
> *You have made him little less than a god,*
> *crowning his head with glory and honour:*
> *you made him master of all you have made,*
> *putting everything in subjection under his feet …*
> *O Lord, our Lord, how majestic is your name in all the earth!'*

In this lies our hope.

# OTHERNESS

## Otherness in God

When I worked for the World Council of Churches my assignments took me to poor areas to 'feel the life' of the people there.

A house in San Miguelito, Panama, was as poor and bare as any I encountered. There, Bill, a reformed drunk and now a lay pastor, conducted a liturgy of the Word. About a dozen people, in their twenties and early thirties, pressed in carrying stools, for the room was almost bare of furniture. They all shared in the service, including the building up of the sermon.

At one point it was clear that Bill was pressing them too hard in emphasising God's presence in the midst of life. 'We know that God is in the thick of things where we are,' they rejoined. 'We believe that. But that is not the whole story. God is also beyond us. We don't know how God can be with us and beyond us. But that is just the way it is.'

Elizabeth Templeton had the insight to publish a book titled *The Strangeness of God*. There will always be features in our encounters with God which it will be difficult to figure out: a nearness giving confidence; an otherness inducing awe. Jesus' life illustrates this. He broke through the hold on people of laws and customs which were supposed to be for their good and which enslaved them. Adultery is a sin which merits death? He refused to condemn an adulterous woman caught in a framed-up situation. The company of publicans and sinners is to be avoided? He sought them out. Appropriate hygienic measures required lepers to be isolated? He touched and healed.

## Otherness in human beings

After her death I once had a dream of Margaret where she looked different from her usual self. Other people might not have recognised her. I knew it was her. I remember telling myself in the dream that the disciples did not at first recognise the risen Jesus, though they had been in his company, day in, day out, for so much of his earthly life. There was a different quality about him though he was the same person. Margaret was my Margaret, but now fulfilled in her risen life: so there was an otherness about her.

But otherness is to be observed and respected in more ordinary levels of life. For years I shared a pew in Gargunnock Church with Miss Miller, a quiet conservative lady who kept herself to herself. Only at the time of her funeral was I given a quite different glimpse of her character. Her mother died when she was ten years old. Her father's work took him away from home. I was told that some arrangement was made for care of the children, she and three younger siblings, by a kindly neighbour. Before long it became clear to her that the provision did not work. She told the other three that she (aged ten) would look after them and rear them. She marched them back to the family house, and there fulfilled her promise. The wee douce lady I knew! It reminded me of Jewish children in concentration camps where young children acted as parents to even younger ones.

The otherness of God and in human beings puts a question mark against inflexible forms of morality. We must be prepared for surprises. In the book *The Cruel Sea*, Liverpool is described as something like a haven of refuge for mariners who diced with danger and death in wartime. The warmth of welcome seemed to be extended mainly by prostitutes and pubs. Would God condemn such a city?

I first came across reference to Sir Richard Burton when I was researching the life and work of R.B. Cunninghame Graham, who ran counter to popular opinion in appreciating the man. True, Burton led a sexually experimental, promiscuous life. But his conduct was based on an appreciation of widely divergent sexual practices in different cultures, which he entered into as fully as was open to someone raised in the Western culture of the Victorian era. To get entry in as natural a way as possible, he mastered fifteen oriental languages. His desire was to understand and appreciate other lifestyles than those favoured in the West. Would God echo the Victorians' condemnation, or 'take him for all in all'?

Homosexuality is against God's will for humankind? Those who say so do justice neither to Old Testament nor New Testament texts. In the Mosaic law measures against homosexuality come with a whole raft of other measures, from purification rituals after childbirth to banning different forms of thread in making cloth. Those who are in for the penny of anti-homosexuality should be in for the pound of observance of the total Mosaic dispensation.

In the New Testament Jesus said, 'You have heard what old-timers have held to … but I say to you …' A greater authority than Moses is present. He also said, 'The things that I do you will do also; and greater things than these shall you do because I go to the Father.' On the road to Emmaus he gave exposition to the Old

Testament so as to illuminate, in the text, 'the things concerning himself' – making it clear by his action that there were plenty of things not concerning himself in that text. What belongs to his way have to be sorted out from those which go against it, through the gift of the Holy Spirit.

Look at the words of Paul. He speaks of homosexuality as being 'against nature'. At the beginning of the letter to the Romans he castigates a range of sins which incur the wrath of God. When he speaks of same-sex intimate relations he uses the words 'natural' and 'unnatural'. He is arguing on the basis of what was held to be proper in his time. Look at 1 Corinthians 11.14,15 – it is taken to be natural that a woman should wear long hair and a man short hair. Tell that to some men footballers and to women who want a short trim! What are thought of as 'natural' and 'unnatural' practices vary in different times and in different cultures. What is natural at any one time is always open to change. If God has so created human life that quite a proportion are homosexual, why should we challenge our Maker? The judgement of society that this is a perversion deliberately adopted to flout society has no evidential validity, it is simply due to a put-down vexation. Let us rejoice in human diversity and learn to understand and appreciate it.

If I were asked who came to mind when 'integrity of life' was thought of, I would say Tom Paine, Fidel Castro, R.B. Cunninghame Graham, if it were male characters which were wanted. If it were female, my thought would not fly to Marilyn Monroe! But in a *Guardian* obituary of August 6th, 1962, Alastair Cooke wrote of her integrity – the woman who advanced to stardom via the casting couch, who got attention with a nude photo in a calendar, whose physical assets kept being promoted?!

Cooke must have called to mind someone shunted from foster home to orphanage, who longed to be out of the pressures of publicity, who was heard to say she would like to be a cleaning woman, whose life was caught and used both in ways of her own choosing and in ways over which she had no control.

When Samuel, acting as king-maker, looked for a successor to Saul among Jesse's sons, Eliab seemed to have the bearing and qualities which made him an obvious choice. But God indicated to Samuel: 'Do not look on his appearance or on the height of his stature … for the Lord does not see as normal mortals see; they look on outward appearance, but the Lord looks on the heart.' So the youngest, David, who had not even been included in the parade of hopeful sons, was chosen (Samuel 1.16).

'The Lord sees as man does not' the otherness which is less apparent.

## Otherness in language

When I was Dean at Selly Oak Colleges, students could come from about fifty countries. They all had to have a reasonable working grasp of English. But we encouraged tutors, if some exercise they had asked for seemed to be substandard, to sit down with the student concerned and find out whether what had been submitted was careless, superficial thinking, or thought which was difficult to express in a language other than their native one. If the original language was essentially oral, exercises could be submitted on tape. Media permitted could include singing and dancing. Those who stumbled and stuttered in one form of articulation could be vividly fluent in another. Their otherness had to be sensitively catered for.

I know the dilemma of finding words which communicate.

When, after my theological training, I went into industry as a manual working labourer-pastor, the French worker-priest movement had not yet started. It was a new venture. Journalists clustered round. I took the step because of pressure from the Holy Spirit. Would this communicate to the press? Through working in my father's butcher's shop I came alongside shop-hands who thought that faith and church were for respectable people, not for the likes of them. It is important to get across, in interviews, what communicates and makes sense. So I majored on the experience of being a young lad helping out a blind father who was a butcher. But I also mentioned God's Spirit. For one thing, that had basic significance. For another, some journalists might have, or have had, experiences which came from some form of pressure from outside the familiar; and my word about the Spirit might resonate, helping people to be aware of 'otherness' in making sense of events.

## Otherness in situations

Otherness in situations which seem to have obstinate, intransigent features may have in store a tiny resource which, beyond all expectation, can split situations open. What bets would have been placed on the long-imprisoned Mandela breaking open apartheid? Or a caretaker Pope such as John XXIII undertaking to update the church by summoning Vatican II? How is it that the demise of Soviet communism cannot be fully explained without taking into account the influence of the Beatles, brought to bear just by doing their stuff? Ideological masters who were at home with dogmatic formulae could not cope with new rhythms! In Guatemala I heard of oppressive authorities who identified and eliminated leaders of basic ecclesial communities – but could not cope with the fact that the most unlikely members would then sprout leadership qualities, much as crabs grow claws. And did not Moses tell God: 'You made a mistake picking on me'?

There is a Spirit at work, untamed, untameable, who keeps springing surprises.

## PURITY: A MEANDER

Christian living has kept being invaded by an understanding of purity which contradicts that held by Jesus and St Paul. It commends keeping life intact, keeping clear of engagement in human concerns where you might get soiled. It commends withdrawal from much of which makes up human life.

Jesus accepted the terms of human life as appropriate for living and proclaiming the Kingdom of God. He required his followers to get soiled. They were to 'bear fruit, fruit which will last'. So they had to be like grains of wheat which needed soiling to produce growth towards harvest. He warned against being like seed which remains intact. It contradicts its purpose by remaining unfruitful.

If dirt sticks, through the hostile reactions to what the followers do for Christ's sake, that has to be taken as part of the discipleship package: 'Blessed are you when people revile you and persecute you and utter all kinds of evil against you falsely, on account of me.' Jesus himself was called 'a gluttonous man and a winebibber'.

He castigated the scribes and Pharisees for their obsessive concern with ritual cleansing to get the non-contaminated front they showed publicly, while concealing corrupt behaviour.

Purity of life, for Paul, had to do with keeping his eye on the objectives for which life was given, allowing nothing from the past or the present to distract him or come in the way. If that meant all kinds of hardship and vilification, so be it. Biblically purity is not to be found in clean-handedness but in single-mindedness.

In the novel *Inés of my Soul* Isabel Allende speaks of Pedro de Valdivia's attraction to the *'beauty and virtue'* of Marina Ortiz de Gaete. Isabel goes on: *'Her family had wanted her protected from contact with the world and wanted her to stay that way.'* Pedro married her. But she would not allow him to touch her intimately and *'ran screaming down the corridors'* when he tried. False purity, based on intactness, ruined the marriage.

Poor Mary, Jesus' mother, is sometimes made an icon of purity, put on a pedestal. The brave lass – who was prepared to be pregnant without benefit of husband; who reared a considerable family partly as a single mum; who was with Jesus right to the crucifixion; who became a believer in his resurrection – can have perpetual virginity attributed to her – as if that were a special honour instead of a contradiction of the evidence and a dishonouring. Where commentators do not go as far as that, they may still bestow on Mary what goes beyond normal human qualities and thus rob humanity of someone who lived and loved, rejoiced and suffered: a life companion who can be called 'Mother of the church' (Pope Paul VI, 1964) without that being an attempt to exaggerate her status but rather to assert that she is with us, not an ideal above us.

To rid us of a false sense of purity we need to look at the biblical use of the words for 'world' and 'flesh'.

James in his epistle speaks of our calling thus: 'Religion that is pure and undefiled before God the Father is this: to care for orphans and widows in their distress and to keep oneself unstained by the world.' So the world can besmirch us! But John 3.16 says: 'God so loved the world that he gave his only Son, so that everyone who believes in him may not perish but have eternal life.' So the world is to be loved! The reality is that life requires the world to be described in two ways. The world can get into the hands of people who pursue their own interests and lusts regardless of God's will for the world. That is a way of death. But God interferes by sending his Son to make possible a world of justice, truth and peace. Jesus, speaking to the Father about his disciples, said: 'They are not *of* the world as I am not *of* the world' – the 'of' suggesting belonging to the world which works in hostility to

God. That world, he says, he had overcome. The way is now free for us to join with Jesus Christ in transforming the world God loves into what it was intended to be.

The word 'flesh' is also used in different ways. It can be used for humanity in general: 'The glory of the Lord shall be revealed and all flesh shall see it together.' The emphasis may be on human frailty: 'All flesh is grass ... the grass withers ...' The word can describe our lower nature 'fleshly lusts'. After Paul has stressed 'flesh and blood cannot inherit God's Kingdom', he indicates how that can change – a perishable body putting on imperishability, a mortal body immortality: for Jesus Christ has overcome the enemy, death, and that has transformed earthly realities.

The word 'flesh' is used for life which is visible and the word 'spirit' for qualities which are unseen. They need not be in contradiction. The spirit can act through the flesh to fulfil God's purposes. They can also be antagonistic, when 'flesh' has the sense of human beings managing life so as to get what they want out of it, regardless of God's will for it. 'Sins of the flesh' are taken to describe sexual sins in popular speech. In Paul's lists these are included but do not dominate – a whole range of human faults and failings is covered.

As early as the book of Leviticus the command is given: 'You shall be holy for I, the Lord your God, am holy.' The core idea in the word 'holy' is separation. But it is clear that 'You shall be holy' does not mean separation from the world but separation *for* God *in* the world.

# LAW AND GRACE

Law needs to have grace lurking in its shadows, underpinning it, to make it fully human. It can be itself a form of grace when it prevents exploitation and protects fragile and vulnerable human beings, other creatures and the environment. But where the letter of the law is adhered to in face of what should be a just and fair ordering of life, grace needs to come in to mitigate the rigour and, at times, humanise the law itself. An example of the need for this is found in Nicaragua where abortion is illegal. Surrounding circumstances are not taken into account. Women who have serious difficulty with a pregnancy, to the extent of a possible death sentence, are allowed to die by pressure from those who declare themselves to be 'pro-life'! Rather than have life saved by an abortion, death is willed on mothers. The law is then without grace.

I personally found grace operating in law courts when I took those who promulgated the Poll Tax to court for promoting bad law (on the basis that bad law is not just to be deplored but to be fought). Those who sat in judgement on my case (I think especially of the Law Lords) had to deal with me as someone who had no legal training and no knowledge of how courts functioned. But they listened intently and sympathetically – as if to discover whether, beyond the technicalities, some wrong was being addressed which deserved attention. They brought to bear not only the requirements of law but the human need for justice. Grace accompanied the administration of law.

Two of my uncles were small farmers in the Dallas, Morayshire region. They never articulated their understanding of law. But from their attitudes and actions I formed a pretty good guess. It was tripartite:

There were creatures which flew or ran over their fields. These were the property of the laird. That was the law of the land.

Such creatures, which fed on these fields, were fair game for the tenant farmer's cooking pot. That was the law of God.

When it came to the bit, you should choose what fights to get into and what to avoid. That was the law of expediency.

I can illustrate.

On one occasion, when I was helping with the harvest on Uncle John and Auntie Nellie's farm, I went out with the gun. I shot a grouse. When I came in sight of the house, I saw a bicycle against the wall which I recognised to be the gamekeeper's. I went down into the harvest field, put the gun under a stook, took a sheaf, pulled out the middle and inserted the grouse. I walked back to the house, all innocence, with a sheaf under my arm. Auntie Nellie was clearly a believer in the law of God. She was delighted to cook the grouse, once the gamekeeper was out of the way.

Something similar can happen when it is not law but discipline which is at stake.

I have been a member of the Iona Community since 1941. George MacLeod had a passionate conviction of the need for a new committed Christian community. But he was also a great individualist and sometimes that got the better of him. I never once accepted decisions which George tried to foist unilaterally on the Community. On the other hand, if the Community made decisions which I did not agree with, I went with them. We were and are a decision-making *body*.

In the early 1940s, George on one occasion decided that we novices were too undisciplined. We were told, one Friday, that, after evening prayers, we should retire to our rooms and shut our doors on the day. (George himself felt free to pound his typewriter into the wee sma' hours.) There was a village dance on Fridays.

I summoned the troops. We closed our doors on the day that evening – and went out of the windows; then danced every dance till 4am. A boat had been sent out to fish. In the largest room in the village we then assembled to have a ceilidh of song, comic recitation and story, while the fish were cooked and passed around. About 7am we dived off the pier to freshen up, climbed back through the windows and, by 7.30am, were ready for another day. You can fight bad law through the courts or by stratagem!

Jesus said that he had not come to abolish the law of Moses but to fulfil it – to fill it out with grace, searching for the deep intention which lay behind inflexible commandments. Thus when the disciples picked grains of corn, rubbed them in their hands, and chewed the kernels, and were compared to millers grinding meal on the Sabbath, he rejected the accusation. The Sabbath was a provision of grace, to give rest from toil and time for reflection and for worship – enhancing human life, not restricting it gracelessly: 'The Sabbath was made for humankind, not humankind for the Sabbath!'

Many blue moons ago I took part in a gathering, in Rome, of representatives of over thirty basic Christian communities from the city and surrounding region. The background of the majority was Roman Catholic. The leadership for the day was in the hands of a Baptist pastor and his people. In an interval I asked some of the Roman Catholics how the 'church-born-from-below' was able to thrive under the shadow of Vatican traditionalists who were uneasy about developments attributed to the Spirit which they could not control. The answer came, 'Oh, we just duck under their arms and get on with the job.'

Sometimes there is a need for confrontation, as I judged there was in opposing the Poll Tax. Sometimes what is needed is to duck under arms and get on with the job. Both can be means of grace in dealing with law and order.

## A MEANDER ROUND GRACE

The Greek word *charis* is used for bodily movement in dance which delights the eye, and also for generous movement in relationships which delights the heart. In each case the source of grace is beyond human attainment, but it conspires to bring out the best in us if we are prepared to offer the best – grace never overwhelms, it pleads and entices but leaves freedom with regard to our response to its plea.

While we were serving in Rosyth, a growing lad, charmed by my Margaret's loveliness and liveliness, asked his mother: 'How can a minister get somebody like that?' – as if, for that category of person, a dowdy alternative would be more fitting!

I was in the Old Quadrangle, leaning over the balustrade with a friend when I was a student at New College. He groaned out loud. I asked if he was ill. 'No,' he replied. 'Married – and that is still on the market!' 'That' was Margaret in a summer frock walking diagonally across the quad. I did not tell him that I was starting to take steps to corner that market.

Grace marked our whole married life. We delighted in one another. We could well never have met! Forres students who went to university most often chose Aberdeen. But to live in a blind man's household can mean that you lack space for yourself – your spare time is so much tied into the work of the shop, reading to him (dad would not learn Braille), and evening engagements such as a prayer meeting or the Literary Society. My main reason for wanting to go to Edinburgh was that the distance provided me with greater freedom to do my own thinking and direct my own life. Margaret, in her last year of school, thought she would have to go into her Auntie Meg's legal business, because her parents could not have afforded university fees. But she was awarded a scholarship as the most promising pupil in the area and that took her to Edinburgh.

We still need not have met. By that time I was in New College and she was in the university. But though my fellow students were a good enough bunch, I wanted a wider and more varied company. So, after classes, I went to the university reading rooms to do study work. In the upper reading room I saw Margaret for the first time, kept an eye on her table, and when someone left, ambled across and happened to be introduced by a mutual friend. Grace overcame hurdles of physical distance.

# A MEANDER ROUND PRAYER

Prayer is no monopoly of those who are religiously inclined. It is a constituent element of human existence. And mountains may give praise to God simply by existing, as they are. Human beings must give them voice. To rejoice in a slave people who escaped from Egypt, 'the slave-pen', the mountains 'skip like rams'. The psalmist does not see praise of God confined to human beings, though we have responsibility to articulate it:

> *Praise the Lord from the earth …*
> *… Mountains and all hills,*
> *fruit trees and all cedars,*
> *wild animals and all cattle,*
> *creeping things and flying birds …*

Recourse to prayer is woven into the fabric of the universe.

There are some for whom prayer is a constituent of life which is drawn on as constantly as lungs draw in air. On one occasion, when I was in the Philippines, I went to meet Momy de la Torre to try to see her son Ed, my friend, who had been jailed under the Marcos dictatorship. I had no authorisation for a visit. As we walked from the bus stop Momy was in communication, but not with me. She was trying, trying to get some direction. As we neared the gate of the prison she seemed to get an answer. She turned and said to me: 'We have to do this straight.' I have written the detail elsewhere of how we got through the outer and inner courtyards without any let or hindrance, quite like the way in which Peter came out of jail.

Others may not even be aware that they are praying! Prayer need not look like prayer; need not be expressed in words. I remember a perceptive journalist who was sent to interview a very promising young football player. All he got was mumbles, not a word worth reporting. The journalist concluded with: 'Where he is articulate is on the football field.' Articulation can take a variety of forms in the ongoing processes of living. The love of my life, Margaret, returned my love with every fibre of her being months before she was able to put that love into words.

God responds to human situations where actual prayer is not clearly involved. So oppressed were the Hebrew people in Egypt under their task-masters that they seemed only to groan and cry out, without shaping their words into prayers. It was enough. God hears cries, and answers cries as well as prayers.

Prayer may be expressed in work. In Ecclesiasticus 38, the writer looks at the upholding of daily life by basic workers – ploughman, engravers, smiths, potters – and concludes that 'their daily work is their prayer' – the thought and expertise invested in it make it not just a labour, not even just a labour of love, but an offering. The will of God is seen to be fulfilled by the way in which their offering moves life forward: 'Without them a city would have no inhabitants ... they sustain the fabric of the world.' I asked a joiner who supplied two doors for me, whose craftsmanship elsewhere in the village I had admired, whether he would rather get a large payment for some rushed and rather substandard work or inadequate payment for work on which he had lavished craftsmanship and extra time. He did not want to answer such a theoretical question. But it was clear from his few stumbling words that he would be fixed on doing the job well, letting nothing come in his way. I am pretty sure he would never have thought of that commitment as having prayer in it.

On one occasion, in Rosyth, I was visiting in the area of small houses popularly called 'Dollytown'. One door on which I knocked was opened by a man whom I at once recognised as the communist/atheist secretary of one of the dockyard trade unions. He said, roughly: 'What are you calling here for? I'm not one of yours.' I said that I was not appointed to a congregation but to Rosyth Parish. So it was in order for me to knock on his door. Equally, it was his door, and he had a right to close it in my face. He exchanged a sentence or two and then closed it. I called one other time.

Later, I was visiting in the same area, and people told me this man was desperate to see me. I went to his door and this time he pulled me in. His wife was seriously ill in hospital. She meant so much to him! We talked about loving relationships. Then he asked me to pray for her, there and then. I said that we had established a good, human relationship – there was no need for him to ask for something beyond his honestly held position. 'Stop your bloody nonsense,' he retorted. 'Get down on your knees here and pray for my wife and myself.' I stopped my bloody nonsense. I got down on my knees beside him. Together we lifted the woman he loved to the God in whom he had said he did not believe.

I would not want to deny him his atheism. It was just that human love (temporarily?) opened a split in the shell within which atheism curled.

# THEOLOGY AND FASHION

One of the many things I loved about Margaret was her taste in clothes. She was very gifted in different needlework arts – sewing, dressmaking, crochet work, knitting. To start with she made frocks for herself and crocheted tops to go with skirts. When the family arrived, knitting had to predominate – and darning. I remember looking at a pair of socks she had darned so neatly that they could have been displayed in a craft exhibition.

She much preferred to have me with her when she was looking for an outfit. Sometimes we would go to different parts of a store and bring possible garments to one another for appraisal. If nothing was just a right match (and at a right price, for we had little to go on) we would go to another store or leave it for another day. To get the right garment at the affordable price Margaret would show great patience, and in the end would succeed. I loved to see her looking her best.

One triumph was the black outfit she got for my sister's wedding. That was spotted by her on her own. I had the occasional triumph. In a small Stirling shop I noted a flame-coloured ballgown which looked her size and turned out to be so. The liquefaction of the slightly different shades was highlighted as she moved. Another time when we were in Geneva I had assignments in Britain and noted that trouser suits were popular there, as they were not with the rather staid Swiss. I risked buying two. I had no problems about measurements (in that regard I was a hands-on person!) but I held my breath. I need not have worried. Margaret loved them and especially favoured a maroon-coloured one.

In discussing fashion, the Countess of Mar and Kellie on one occasion spoke to me about the kind of clothes which she looked for: good quality, right colour and good cut without being ostentatious. She knew that I had an eye for clothes. I asked if she had considered the theological basis for making choices. She had not, and was immediately interested. I said that there were positive and negative implications. The positive was simple. If we are made in the image of God we should look the part, and not look like something which has crawled out of a primaeval swamp. The negative implications were found with people who did not think that the image of God expressed their claim to significance and looked for clothes to provide significance for their life. They might follow every new fashion, discarding perfectly attractive garments in order to keep up with the Joneses, often putting themselves seriously into debt or becoming spendaholics. Money beyond basic needs would accordingly be selfishly expended when it could have gone to relieve poverty and distress around their doors or in different parts of the world. The attention given to enhancement of appearance could fill the mind, become an obsession which drove out imaginative and responsible thinking about life's larger concerns. Did not Jesus say: 'Life is more than food and the body more than clothing.'?

## OH TO BE WRINKLE-FREE

A good deal of advertising time on television is taken up with the advocacy of potions which, it is claimed, will abolish or at least reduce the development of wrinkles. A great deal of money is spent on meeting what is perceived as a desirable and desired objective.

There are programmes which examine and assess the promises and effects of plastic surgery, where the face or other body parts go under the knife in attempts to remedy supposed defects and improve personal appearance.

Underlying the claims of promoters and customers are theological perceptions, good and bad.

Margaret was born with a birthmark. It was removed early. It could have spread and given distress. Surgical removal was a blessing. In my day, a boy in the class had a cleft lip. No cure was then known or at least attempted. Much more serious disfigurements can now be dealt with, at least in countries which are affluent enough. A good National Health Service is a concrete theological statement that everyone who lives is made in the image of God, whatever their wealth or social status; and are due attentive care.

But – the removal of wrinkles? Are these not signs that we have lived and loved, failed and succeeded, suffered and won through? Are these not the equivalent to medals which recognise human maturity? In El Salvador I was within a whisker of falling into the hands of the death squads. In the Philippines, when Marcos tried to hide the tortures and assassinations of his seamy regime, I was within half a whisker of being caught and jailed. Should I covet a face as smooth and feature-less as a baby's bum – yes, wrinkle-free, but lacking any signs of maturity? Audrey Hepburn was wiser. She must have been one of the most photographed people in the world, and she photographed so well! Yet her favourite photo was when she was UN ambassador for children, caught unprepared with a child hanging like a large necklace round her neck. She said then that every wrinkle she had was earned – and not even one should be airbrushed out.

On an occasion when a group of apprentices spent some days at Scottish Churches House, we took them to see a double programme of Sean Connery films, *Dr. No* and *From Russia with Love*. The next day they had an assessment. On being asked: 'What do you think of the Bond women?' they answered with tongues moving round lips: 'Lush, man, lush!' 'If you had the chance to marry one would you take it?' I asked. Back came a unanimous: 'Not on your life, sir'; and the biggest and toughest, who was looked on by the others as a natural leader, added: 'When I marry I want someone like my granny.' Grannies can be loving. Grannies can be fun. But don't they inevitably have wrinkles?

Jesus saw that obsessive fretting to give the appearance of being a holy person, such as 'Holy Willie' whom Burns cartooned, was another form of self-concern. It is the whole life which matters, not just appearance; and sometimes wrinkles can give expression to its depth and quality.

O the delightful wrinkles round the eyes and the mouth and on the brow of a beloved one!

# THE IMPORTANCE OF FOOD-SHARING

Jesus made food-sharing central.

There is the case of feeding of thousands. Zacchaeus asked Jesus to stay at his house (a typical man, he assumed that there would be enough food for an extra one at the table!). What Jesus left for all later generations was a simple meal which allowed him to give himself to us and allows us, by the act of eating and drinking, to receive him into our beings, providing a communion in community.

I found the importance of food-sharing when I worked for the World Council of Churches and was asked to be responsible for the 'Participation in Change' programme. I asked for a rethink of how WCC studies were tackled. When an Assembly was held and studies for future work were identified, the usual approach was to get a group of people to 'have a go' at each study and send the results all over the world, seeking reactions and responses. I pointed out that those who formed such groups were mainly Europeans within reach, and Americans (they had money for travel costs). What came back from the ends of the earth was shaped up and issued as a *world* study, whereas a) a Western stamp had been put on it to start with b) there were parts of the world, e.g. islands of the Pacific, which were hardly given time even to respond because mail took so long to be delivered. I also said that studies seemed to attract intellectuals whereas they should be a resource for all kinds of concerned people. If the option for the poor were to be taken seriously, it would be good to concentrate on how the poor were making out today participating in so much change in the world.

I was given clearance to reverse the usual process, and to go and live with the poor in different parts of the world, listen to their stories, hear how their faith helped them to cope with drastic change, and bring all that back for the instruction of the rest of the church.

To do this I sent a message ahead of me wherever possible. It indicated that I would not be staying in a hotel – could I get a corner of a shanty to curl up in at night and would they share with me some of their food?

Identification of this kind, even if it were just for 4 or 5 days, produced a trust which meant that their life-stories came tumbling out as would never have happened had I visited from a hotel. I got used to sleeping in my clothes; and my constitution proved adequate to cope with whatever was their own ration for the day.

One discovery concerned people who did not have enough to eat. To share what was available (four potatoes in the Dominican Republic, a large plate of vegetable soup in a Pentecostal centre in Venezuela come to mind as food for the day) reversed the situation. Where those I stayed with may have been at the receiving end of handouts, they became the hosts: I was their guest. That gave them a dignity which seemed to mean more to them than food – as did a realisation that the World Council of Churches could be enlightened by what they were making of life amid all the changes they experienced.

## SEXUALITY AND SPIRITUALITY

What was God thinking of in making us sexual beings? If it had just been a matter of propagation of the species we could have been made to accrete, as is the case with bulbs. Sexuality opens the door to penetration of and by others, both that interpenetration in social relationships in which male and female contributions can make perceptions and decisions more rounded and complete if they are thoughtfully brought together, and that deep penetration which marks sexual intercourse.

Sexuality opens the door to endemic male assertiveness. It opens the door to sexual trafficking. It opens the door to rape, both on a domestic scale and as a device of armies to humiliate, oppress and enslave others. Is there any clearer rejection of the biblical testimony that human beings are made in the likeness of God than forced entry into the precious core of being of other persons, that core of being which should be kept intact or only yielded freely to the entry of a joyfully invited beloved one?

What was God thinking of?

We must distinguish between 'the sensuous' and 'the sensual' forms of life. The former is defined as 'appreciative of qualities perceived by the senses'; the latter as indicating 'excessive indulgence in sexual pleasures' or being 'unduly inclined to gratification of the senses'. In the former, experience of the senses is relished, appreciated as a marvellous gift accompanying bodily creation. In the latter the senses are allowed to take charge, ruling the person who should be in control.

O the crowning of our humanity which the senses can supply! Kisses on honeyed breath speak a loved one's glad invitation. Fingertips luxuriate in silken skin, and a body comes alive in welcome. Bodies interpenetrate deliciously … to the point where the lover and the beloved pour their beings into one another, affirming their unity, crowning it. That deep affirmation of one another as partners lightens and enlarges their togetherness when they tackle the more humdrum claims of ordinary life.

What does it say about God that such unity can be experienced? It speaks of God's delight in us and God's desire that we delight in one another. It is a sign of God the Chancer, who is prepared to take risks which appal the angels – for in sexual relationships so much can go wrong. Love does not play safe.

Our rational faculty exercises a mandate to patrol the senses to prevent them from being thoughtlessly, carelessly expended, lest we invade one another's beings wantonly. Rape is the extreme example of such invasions. Want of control can bring lesser but still heartbreaking damage. Courtship is a time when a sussing out takes place – allowing possible life-partners to judge their capacity to live lovingly together before consummating a union. Here the rational faculty enables the best interests of both partners to be served. We owe to it mature choices.

But the rational faculty is not fully rational unless it knows how to give way and stand aside at the appropriate point. This will not be an abandonment but a fulfilment of its responsibility.

Think of Wesley's *'till we cast our crowns before Thee, lost in wonder, love and praise'*. It is the promise of God that our life will be crowned beyond death. But our reason is aware that the crown is not of merit but of God's sheer grace. It is reasonable, therefore, to make the gesture of casting crowns down before God. At that point reason wisely stands aside. *'Lost in wonder, love and praise'* is spiritual orgasm, abandonment to God.

Love calls for discipline as well as mutual abandonment. When discipline is exercised, love matures. It enables partners to pull together through thick and thin. Three Greek words indicate distinctive types of loving relationship. *Eros* speaks of relationships in which the senses are aflame. *Agape* expresses the warm relationship in committed communities where friendship and respect are uniting factors – Paul urged Christians in their gatherings to greet one another with a holy kiss. *Philadelphia* signals a relationship such as might be found between brothers and sisters in a loving family.

The wider relationships will not be so intense but will still be productive of unselfish concern for one another's good. They will also be sexual, in that different sexes have different contributions to make to our common life. Let me illustrate from my own experience.

In Selly Oak Colleges, the head of the Social Work Department came to me with a problem. He had to include two classes on sexuality in the programme for a term. He was scared of tackling the subject – would I be willing to step in? I agreed and he warned, 'You will have to catch their interest from the word "go" or you will lose them.' So I started off: 'I have a sexual relationship with my secretary, and she is a married woman.' They sat up – all ears! Their interest continued even after I pointed out that sexual relationship was so often spoken about as if it meant physical congress, when sexual difference produces different emphases, different ways of looking at life which can contribute to one another. I might have illustrated from work with Denise, my secretary in the World Council of Churches. We collaborated in developing the programme 'Participation in Change'. At one point she said that she thought a contact with Iroquois communities in Canada needed to be picked up and followed through more definitely. I saw that she had been thinking this through. She was the one to develop that further! We agreed that she should do so. Sometimes a difference in sexuality results in different aspects being emphasised, leading to different angles of understanding and interpretation. If these are honoured and brought together, the result can be an enrichment of perceptions and conclusions.

A vivid example came when Margaret and I retired. The Mission Societies and Boards of Britain asked us together to continue to visit basic Christian communities in different parts of the world and bring back insights for the renewal of the church in Britain. We agreed to take separate notes. When it was time to share these, we sorted them into main points, sub-points and a few observations. No table was big enough to make an assessment. On the floor, against the wall of a room, we laid these out, each telling the other, in the process, why we had made our choices. Once that was done, we looked at one another in astonishment, wondering if we had been through the same experiences at all! In the end our different appraisals of situations and different emphases added up to a much better three-dimensional appreciation of our experiences. We were so much of one mind; yet different things were observed, different angles of interest developed, different emphases laid. When these were put together we produced *Wind and Fire: the Spirit Reshapes the Church in Basic Christian Communities*.

Alastair McIntosh once observed to me that he considered sexuality and spirituality to be different sides of the same coin. I responded that, in my judgement, they were on the same side. At the very beginning of the Bible the word used for the sexual intercourse of human beings is the same word as for entering into committed relationship with God.

Love is life's key and crown.

## ATONEMENT

Over centuries thinkers have struggled to understand how, with integrity, God could be at one with humanity, with the blemished record of our trusteeship so manifest and our failures in responsible, loving relationships so irrefutable. God does not ignore the way in which those to whom have been given this trust and task respond to the challenge. So how can God do other than what is expressed in the story of Noah: 'I have determined to make an end of all flesh because the earth is full of violence …'? Something has happened to change the situation so that there can be at-one-ment in spite of all the bad omens. How are we to understand the change?

With Noah it comes in the form of a covenant: 'I'll be your God, you be my people.' A covenant is the basis on which, in the Old Testament, a Day of Atonement is observed to put right with God relationships which had been fractured. The ritual related only to sins of omission and ignorance. After a cleansing of the sanctuary, confession of the sins of the people, priests and laity alike, was made by the High Priest. He did so with his hands on the head of a goat, symbolically transferring to the animal those sins. The animal was then driven into the wilderness bearing away the sins of the people and restoring the covenant relationship. The writer to the Hebrews points out that this may express the people's guilt and longing to live truly God's way; but it did not effect the change. It took Jesus Christ's sacrificial life to do that in real terms.

Those who are in the Hebrew/Christian tradition at times become very conscious of having let God down, and long for some means of making amends which will restore a true relationship expressed by a change in the way we live. Life which has gone awry needs to be offered back to God and put right.

The writer to the Hebrews sums up the New Testament conviction that Jesus Christ, by his life, death and resurrection, achieved this in a real way to replace all figurative attempts to do so.

The hymn writer puts it:

*'Bearing shame and scoffing rude,*
*in my place, condemned, he stood.'*

There are examples of people standing in for others who have received a death warrant. *A Tale of Two Cities* provides an example in literature of what sometimes happened in real life. But how can that quality of life stand in for us and become ours?

'In my place' can express a substitution theory of atonement. Jesus Christ took the rap which we merited. How? At times it was thought that an angry God had to be appeased. But that assumes a different God from the one Jesus Christ called 'Father'.

We are in deep waters here. Let me try to tease this out. Jesus accepted the conditions and terms of a fully human life. Philippians 2 declares he became not only human, but a *doulos*, a 'slave' or a 'nothing'. He experienced torture and death which identifies him not only with humanity in general but with those who are most despised, most rejected and counted of no worth. He willingly came alongside those who suffer the greatest violence, dredging the depths of human brutality. So he experienced human life at its worst. 'He knew what was in humanity.' The word 'knowing' in the Bible includes more than information. It includes experience in exposure to realities. So Jesus was not only human. He was the second Adam, the definitive human being who, having known all that human beings experience, can be called the Son of Man, essential humanity.

But how can some such way of living as his be made ours?

Jesus lived with others, making visible in the way he lived the difference it would make to the world to take God's way. But he did more.

He left one sacrament which allowed us, in baptism, to discard an old life and rise to a new one; and one which allowed us, through blessed bread and wine, to take into our very being the life which he manifested, to 'cover' our own.

William Bright's hymn for communion puts it simply and effectively:

*'Look, Father, look on his anointed face*
*and only look on us as found in him.'*

The water of baptism is not mere water, the bread and wine of Holy Communion are not mere bread and wine. They are invested with a reality to change and nourish new life. Just as was my mother's wedding ring. She lost it once. What a frantic search that inspired! If you had said: 'I'll replace it' or 'I'll give you 100 times its value in gold' your offer of help would have been rejected out of hand. There was just one ring which sealed the pledge to lifelong love which dad and she had made. After much searching she found it. We breathed a sigh of relief.

Of course we can go back on our covenant, 'discard the ring'. But then we are turning against the change needed if we are to accept the move from a single life to a shared life.

Jesus let his disciples into his understanding of what this relationship implied in his prayer to the Father (John 17.20–23):

*'May they all be one; as you, Father, are in me and I in you, so also may they be*
*in us, that the world may believe that you sent me. The glory which you gave*
*me I have given to them that they may be one as we are one; I in them and you*
*in me, may they be perfectly one. Then the world will know that you sent me,*
*and that you loved them as you loved me.'*

# SUCCESS: A MEANDER

The desire to be a success in life is strong, whether that means to get the approval and applause of an intimate company or to be a 'name' recognised nationally and internationally. What is true of persons is also true of institutions and corporations (note how oil companies advertise their 'green' credentials).

But what is success? One person's success may be another's impoverishment. So we need to examine what genuine, creative success consists of – success which is not like a seesaw where some can go up only if others go down (both in the eyes of the world and in reality).

'The world' is spoken of in quite contrasting ways in the Bible. A warning not to take its ways is given in 1 John 2.15,16: 'Do not love the world or the things in the world. The love of the Father is not in those who love the world; for all that is in the world – the desire of the flesh, the desire of the eyes, the pride in riches – comes not from the Father but from the world.' This kind of 'success' is destructive.

A positive view of the world is given in the Gospel of John 2.16,17: 'God so loved the world that he gave his only Son, so that everyone who believes in him may not perish but may have eternal life. God did not send the Son into the world to condemn the world, but in order that the world might be saved through him.'

It might look as if this provides two quite contrasting views of the world in which we live. John 1:10 may clarify. There it is said of Jesus Christ: 'He was in the world, and the world was made through him, yet the world did not know him.' We are dealing with a world which is destined to be transformed in justice, truth and peace after the manner of Jesus' word and works, but which can also use the freedom it is given to set its own agenda in rejection of that way of ordering life. There is one kind of world to fight for and another kind to oppose. The search for success will fall into one category or the other.

Take the three things warned against in 1 John 2.16:

a) The desire of the flesh: In common speech 'fleshly lust' tends to be thought of as sexual in character. In the original Hebrew it refers to the whole being 'deprived of the Spirit of God, dominated by the appetites', as one biblical dictionary puts it. Success which depends on a dominating power which deprives and crushes others must be forsworn by the People of the Way. 'Whoever wants to be first must be last of all and servant of all' (Mark 9.35).

b) The desire of the eyes: This refers to any attractive person or proposition which may be reached for – other people's wives, mansions, yachts, flashy lifestyles to impress the Joneses, prestigious appointments – if these are distractions from the purpose for which our lives are entrusted: for God knows what is looked for from our lives, which vaunting ambitions may conceal: 'If your eye is healthy, your whole body will be full of light' (Matthew 6.11).

c) The pride in riches: Jesus said bluntly that it is impossible to serve God and Mammon, i.e. piling up of possessions which robs others and distracts from the service for which life is given. We are called to seek first the Kingdom of God and God's right way. All needful things will be given as well.

Jesus told a story about worldly success and failure (Dives and Lazarus, Luke 16. 19–31). The rich man had power; he was in a control position. Even after death he expected Lazarus to be dispatched to serve his need. He satiated his eye, delighting in fine linen clothing and expensive provender. He made no attempt to share his riches, leaving Lazarus to be famished, longing for scraps from his table. A position of power, an eye for the gifts of opulence, a failure to share riches to alleviate distress marked him out from Abraham – who with his flocks and herds was himself never short of a penny or two! Abraham had Lazarus held close, in contrast to Dives' distancing of him. Jesus reminded hearers that success in this world has no bearing on God's final verdict on our lives. Dives failed, for all his privileges.

Think of those in prominent positions who virtually dictate their own salaries and bonuses by belonging to a coterie who over-estimate the worth of their work. No objective measurement of their contribution to society in relation to other kinds of work is made.

Moreover it takes an extensive community with varied gifts to sustain those who so enrich themselves. Show me the 'self-made man' who is not utterly dependent on others! In sleep he is indebted to air and lungs which together keep him alive, and receives power to get his body moving – from quite outside his own contriving! He pushes aside sheets of Egyptian cotton, coverings of Australian wool from a bed made of Scandinavian timber, and puts his feet on the floor of a room in a house he did not build – in hock to an international community before he even starts the day. What justification does he have to ask for more than a modest share of available resources to sustain life?

In the parable of the rich fool, who, to house surplus grain, built more barns, Jesus illustrates the stupidity as well as the injustice of piling up resources beyond what is needed to sustain life. You can't take it with you! Moreover your selfishness will come under God's judgement. Success comes from being 'rich in the sight of God', genuine success being related to developing life constructively to share in the fulfilment of the promise of Revelation 11.15: 'The kingdoms of this world become the Kingdom of our Lord and of his Christ.'

In small and large ways this transformation can be forwarded. I have mentioned in this book that in the Iona Community we have an economic discipline which reminds us that life and the resources to live are a trust, not a possession. In relation to this, the staff on Iona get the same pay. A Warden/minister is paid the same as a cook or a housekeeper.

Margaret had a nose for identifying what we should tackle at each stage of life – and it never depended on advancement in status or in financial provision. At one point in our ministry in Rosyth a representation from the Kirk Session came to me and said, with triumph in their voices, that they had met informally and decided to raise my salary. I thanked them for their thoughtfulness but said they had not quite got it right. They were *offering* that increase. Since Margaret and I had no intention of living on an income which was beyond the means of basic workers in the dockyard, would they tell us what rises in wages had happened around that time and thus enable us to make up our minds. It turned out that dockyard rises were commensurate with their offer, so we accepted happily and gratefully.

The Mastercraftsman knows how the world is designed to work. Apprentices to the Kingdom of God are successful when they learn the craft, whatever part of the whole work is allocated to them as their own particular assignment.

# DANCING FROM LENT INTO EASTER

The TV programme *Strictly Come Dancing* provides a basis for understanding the relationship of Lent to Easter. Hopefuls involved have to undertake a demanding discipline of training. It is hard going for tyros but also for their professional partners, who have to teach them new skills of movement and posture, and hone these to provide a quality of performance. Then they have to take to the floor. They have to take that risk.

Sydney Carter participated in the new hymn-writing project in Scottish Churches House in the 1960s. In the hymn 'Lord of the Dance', he alludes to the practice of the morality-controllers in Jesus' time:

> *'I danced for the Scribe and the Pharisee*
> *but they would not dance and they wouldn't follow me ...'*

The Lord of the Dance had appeared in history. He found strict religious people preoccupied with the old religious laws. They were obsessed with getting their moral footwork right, so that no judge could fault them. Called into partnership by the Lord of the Dance, they would not risk taking to the floor. That was a hazard they dodged.

Jesus affirmed the need for practice. He called the Twelve into a learning experience. They also found it hard going though rewarding. But practising and practising was a preparation for taking to the floor in a new dance of life. Jesus put it this way in a message to Herod: 'I am casting out demons and performing cures today and tomorrow and on the third day I finish my work.' With him the work of incarnation had a term. The time for practice ended in the toughest test of all. It was the final oblation of self-giving: 'I, if I be lifted up, will draw all sorts into partnership.' On the third day he took to the floor, dancing through all time and space to the music of the spheres.

The Lord of the Dance catches into his flow all those who risk lively participation:

> *'I'll live in you, if you'll live in me.*
> *I am the Lord of the Dance,' said he.*

As I see it, the difference between Fred Astaire's partnership with Ginger Rogers and his other partnerships has not to do with accuracy of footwork but with the flow of the dance which they achieved. There is sacrifice and risk in making that flow possible. Fred was a perfectionist and would endlessly work and rework steps till he got it right. Ginger ruefully reminded us that she had to dance backwards, and in high heels – the ending of a dance ascending stairs, left her, at the top, with shoes lined with blood. All the rigorous discipline finds its reward as it pours into impressive movement.

Lent is a time for honing spiritual practice, according to what life allows to be possible. Milton in 'On His Blindness' asks: *'Does God exact day-labour, light deni'd?'* And answers: *'They also serve who only stand and wait.'* The mother with ten children will have little space, as will the father or teenager who endlessly looks for work. Prayer may be done on a bus, faith be expressed in a last crust to a neighbour, hope in simply not giving up in face of pain and sorrow, peace in fighting for trade justice. In the end we come like ski-jumpers to the take-off point. Safety thrown to the winds, abandoning ourselves to the dance of life with the One who is risen.

# SOURCES, ACKNOWLEDGEMENTS AND NOTES

1.  *The Wealth of Nations*, Adam Smith, Penguin Classics, p.358

2.  'The defibrillator worked – now for the intensive care', Polly Toynbee, *The Guardian*, 14 October, 2008

3.  Polly Toynbee, ibid

4.  *Untold Stories*, Alan Bennett, Faber and Faber, Profile Books, p.480

5.  *Immanuel*, Hans-Ruedi Weber, World Council of Churches, 1984

6.  Hans-Ruedi Weber, ibid

7.  The Queen and the Rebels, Ugo Betti, *Penguin Plays: Three European Plays*, 1969, pp.147, 148. Originally translated by Henry Reed, 1956

8.  *American Human Development Report, 2008-2009*, Columbia University Press

9.  'How Israel brought Gaza to the brink of humanitarian catastrophe', Avi Shlaim, *The Guardian*, 7th January, 2009

10. 'Leaked rules detail rewards and penalties at Guantánamo', Ewen MacAskill, *The Guardian*, 16 November, 2007

11. Information from 'Cuba exports health', Hernando Calvo Ospina, *Le Monde Diplomatique* (English edition), August 2006

12. 'Cuba exports health', Hernando Calvo Ospina, *Le Monde Diplomatique* (English edition), August 2006

13. Hernando Calvo Ospina, ibid.

14. Information from 'Cuba exports health', Hernando Calvo Ospina, *Le Monde Diplomatique* (English edition), August 2006

15. Clearly Cyrus the Great is not included in these leaders of the earth, for he *did* let his prisoners go home.

16. 'The King's Breakfast', *When We Were Very Young*, A.A. Milne, illustrated by E.H. Shepard, Methuen, London, 1924

17. 'The birth: Hush! Watch! Hear! (a carol)' © Stainer and Bell. Used by permission of Ian M. Fraser

18. 'The wild card' © Stainer and Bell. Used by permission of Ian M. Fraser

19. *The Gospel of Mark*, William Barclay, St Andrew Press, p.50

20. *The Battle of the Birds and Other Celtic Tales*, Marion Lochhead, The Mercat Press, 1981

21. *A Time for Trumpets*, Nansie Blackie, St Andrews Press, p.143

22. '2000 Years of Jesus, 20 Years of Romero: a fraternal circular letter', Pedro Casaldaliga www.servicioskoinonia.org/Casaldaliga/cartas/january2000.htm

23. Quoted in '2000 Years of Jesus, 20 Years of Romero: a fraternal circular letter', Pedro Casaldaliga

24. 'Thy Kingdom Come', by Ted Schmidt, *The Social Edge: A Monthly Social Justice and Faith Webzine*, October 11, 2006, www.thesocialedge.com

25. *The Catholic Church and the New Churches in Latin America*, Clodovis Boff www.sedos.org/english/boff_1.html

26. Clodovis Boff, ibid

27. 'With God's Army', Stuart Jeffries, *The Guardian*, 17 December, 2008

*Some of the pieces in this book have appeared previously, in different versions, in Open House magazine: A Scottish Religious Magazine of Comment, Opinion and Reflection (www.open-house-scot.co.uk), in Coracle: the magazine of the Iona Community, and in the Iona Community e-zine (www.iona.org.uk).*

# THE IONA COMMUNITY IS:

- An ecumenical movement of men and women from different walks of life and different traditions in the Christian church
- Committed to the gospel of Jesus Christ, and to following where that leads, even into the unknown
- Engaged together, and with people of goodwill across the world, in acting, reflecting and praying for justice, peace and the integrity of creation
- Convinced that the inclusive community it seeks must be embodied in the community it practises

Together with its staff, the community is responsible for:

- The islands residential centres of Iona Abbey, the MacLeod Centre on Iona, and Camas Adventure Centre on the Ross of Mull

and in Glasgow:
- The administration of the Community
- Work with young people
- A publishing house, Wild Goose Publications
- Its association in the revitalising of worship with the Wild Goose Resource Group

The Iona Community was founded in Glasgow in 1938 by George MacLeod, minister, visionary and prophetic witness for peace, in the context of the poverty and despair of the Depression. Its original task of rebuilding the monastic ruins of Iona Abbey became a sign of hopeful rebuilding of community in Scotland and beyond. Today, it consists of about 280 Members, mostly in Britain, and 1500 Associate Members, with 1400 Friends worldwide. Together and apart, the community 'follows the light it has, and prays for more light'.

*For information on the Iona Community contact:*
*The Iona Community, Fourth Floor, Savoy House,*
*140 Sauchiehall Street, Glasgow G2 3DH, UK.*
*Phone: 0141 332 6343*
*admin@iona.org.uk; www.iona.org.uk*

*For enquiries about visiting Iona, please contact:*
*Iona Abbey, Isle of Iona, Argyll PA76 6SN, UK.*
*Phone: 01681 700404*

# ALSO BY IAN M FRASER

## Reinventing Theology as the People's Work

Ian M Fraser, a member of the Iona Community, wrote Reinventing Theology as the People's Work in 1980 for two specific conferences that were to take place in the 1980s. Since then, the ideas it puts forward have become relevant in a much wider context and this book has helped to raise interest in people's theology worldwide. Its underlying conviction is that just as ministry belongs to more than just the clergy, so does the task of theologising belong to all and not just to the professional theologian. Doing theology goes hand in hand with Christian living, and reflecting on faith accompanies Christian discipleship.

With an MA and BD with distinction in Systematic Theology, Ian Fraser entered industry in 1942 as the first of what became a worker-priest/pastor movement. Far from abandoning the ministry – an accusation levelled against him at the time – he was in fact searching for authentic ministry and a more relevant theology. For him, the concern of this book has been a lifelong preoccupation.

ISBN 9781905010011

## The Way Ahead
### *Grown-up Christians*

Ian Fraser has walked alongside slum dwellers in India and Haiti; Nicaraguan and Cuban revolutionaries; priests, nuns and catechists facing arrest and/or death in Central and South America; small farming and fishing communities in the Philippines … His life has been a search for the vision and reality of a church in which all voices are heard and all parts of Christ's body are included. One place where he found such a model was in the underground church in Eastern Europe during the Communist era. He writes about that discovery here, among other life experiences.

This is a book for anyone who cares about where the church is heading. Will the Christian church live or die? What is the way ahead? Perhaps the church will live – if it has the courage and humility to take Ian Fraser's inclusive message to heart.

ISBN 9781905010257

## Living a Countersign
*From Iona to basic Christian communities*

Ian Fraser has first-hand knowledge and experience of basic Christian communities. At the time of the first publication of this book, in 1990, he had gained more than 30 years' experience of visiting and making personal contact with such communities around the world, through his work with the World Council of Churches, subsequently as Dean and Head of the Department of Mission at Selly Oak Colleges, and then as he and his wife Margaret built the basic Christian communities' resource centre at Scottish Churches House in Dunblane.

Basic Christian communities need to be understood in terms of their historical roots, their distinctive features and their experience of struggle. Ian Fraser starts by tracing that part of the rooting system which derives from the founding of the Iona Community in Scotland in the 1930s. He then draws upon various communities' own words to describe essential characteristics of their life, and goes on to offer some examples of their struggles and pointers to their significance. In an appendix he examines traditional marks of the church to demonstrate that the basic Christian communities are living a renewed orthodox faith, with a life-giving quality which is full of the promise of renewal for traditionalist churches.

ISBN 9781905010493

## Strange Fire
*Life stories and prayers*

Inspiring and thought-provoking, this book brings together ninety stories from Ian Fraser's many years among Christian communities around the world. They bring to life the profound faith of ordinary people, often in extremes of hardship or danger. Each story finishes with a prayer or reflection which allows us to link the stories with those of our own daily lives.

*'This is a book for people who pray and people who find prayer difficult . . . a book for people who want to be assured that God is still at work in his world – and in ways they had not dreamed!' Stuart McWilliam, minister '. . . reality and vision powerfully intermingled . . . an eloquent, dynamic and very personal statement of Christian belief.'*

Tom Fleming, actor and broadcaster

ISBN 9780947988678

Wild Goose Publications, the publishing house of the Iona Community established in the Celtic Christian tradition of Saint Columba, produces books, CDs and digital downloads on:

- holistic spirituality
- social justice
- political and peace issues
- healing
- innovative approaches to worship
- song in worship, including the work of the Wild Goose Resource Group
- material for meditation and reflection

For more information, please contact us at:

Wild Goose Publications
Fourth Floor, Savoy House
140 Sauchiehall Street,
Glasgow G2 3DH, UK

Tel. +44 (0)141 332 6292
Fax +44 (0)141 332 1090
e-mail: admin@ionabooks.com

or visit our website at
www.ionabooks.com
for details of all our products and online sales